Congress Square, Portland, December 1939: Trolley turns off Congress Street, sign urges 'Use Electricity.' In Europe, World War II has begun

The Light from the River

This book is dedicated to
the Central Maine Power Company employees
of the past ten decades who have lost their lives
while defending their country
or while working to provide
safe and reliable electric service for customers.

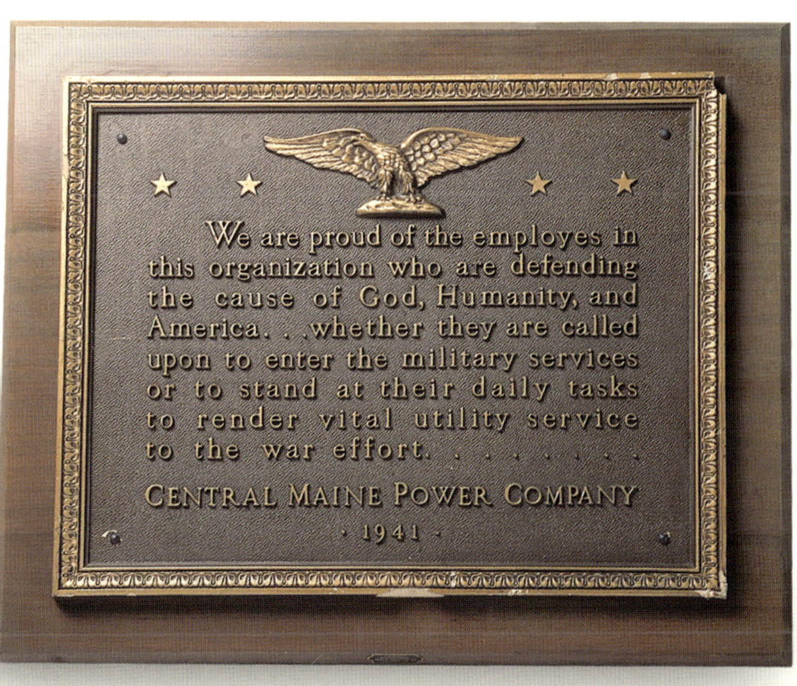

Irwin, Clark T., Jr., 1947-
The Light from the River: Central Maine Power's First Century of Service, 1899-1999
p. cm.
Includes bibliographical references.
ISBN 0-9665645-1-0
ISBN 0-9665645-0-2 (Softcover version)
1. History—United States. 2. Business history—United States. 3. Electric industry—United States. 4. History—Maine.
Library of Congress Catalog Card Number 99-63709

Written and edited by Clark T. Irwin, Jr., and designed by David A. Guillemette for Central Maine Power Company, a subsidiary of CMP Group, Incorporated.

Printed in the United States of America by Letter Systems/Knowlton & McLeary, Hallowell, Maine.

For further information, please write to:
Corporate Communications Department
Central Maine Power Company,
83 Edison Drive, Augusta, Maine 04336.

Table of contents

STATE OF MAINE
OFFICE OF THE GOVERNOR
1 STATE HOUSE STATION
AUGUSTA, MAINE
04333-0001

ANGUS S. KING, JR.
GOVERNOR

Foreword by Gov. Angus S. King, Jr.

November 7, 1999, marks the 100th birthday of the company now known as Central Maine Power. As in any long life, the passing years have brought triumph and tragedy, strain and reconciliation, retrenchment and progress.

CMP has not escaped controversy, and has at times been obliged to rethink its decisions and pay the costs of error. At other times, CMP has been the instrument of public policies that have had unintended consequences for Maine's economy and citizens. But as this book also shows, CMP has a good record of service for more than half a million customers in one of the most rural states in America, and has cooperated with Maine regulators and lawmakers in crafting innovative regulatory approaches that have served as models for other states. There are lessons on both sides of the ledger.

Even after the State-mandated sale of its generating assets and the start of retail electric competition in March 2000, Central Maine Power Company will continue to provide the vital services of transmitting and distributing electric energy, of maintaining and improving the electric infrastructure, and of making repairs required by accidents and natural disasters like the floods of 1936, the fires of 1947, the hurricanes of 1954, and the ice storms of 1998.

The people, past and present, of CMP have played an important role in the economic and social development of Maine. I salute them on this centennial, and wish them success in a second century of service to the people of Maine.

Angus King

PHONE: (207) 287-3531(Voice)

PRINTED ON RECYCLED PAPER

FAX: (207) 287-1034

(207) 287-6548 (TTY)

Central Maine Power
ELECTRIC SHOP
ICE CREAM

POWER

The Light from the River

Central Maine Power's
First Century of Service, 1899-1999

The River

Water gauge from Messalonskee power house

Water for power, Oakland →

November 1899. Fed by ancient springs and autumn rains, the cold waters of the Messalonskee Stream flow out of the Belgrade Lakes and run 11 miles from their source, through the 1,600-person town of Oakland, Maine, before pouring into the Kennebec River, pathway to the Atlantic.

The stream drops 210 feet between its source and the Kennebec. Some 120 feet of that fall, and much of that potential energy, occurs in Oakland. So starting around 1790, men built dams there.

Four dams slow the Messalonskee stream's passage through Oakland. Shops and mills tap the power of the water to cut wood, card wool, grind grain, tan leather, build carriages, and make tools. Oakland is a force in the tool trade: the peavey used by generations of lumbermen was invented and made here, and Oakland leads the world in scythe-making between 1850 and 1960.[1]

The Oakland peavey

As at thousands of other American manufacturing plants, water turns shafts to power the belt-driven machinery in the shops. Except for steel rods and leather belts that replaced wooden shafts and gears, the use of water power

← Overleaf: Scouting a stream, the founders and colleague early 1900s has not essentially changed from its application to grinding grain, beating fibers or metal, or tanning hides in 12th-century European mills.[2] Steam power, fueled by coal or wood, has been growing nationally, especially since the 1870s. But for a place like Oakland, it is hard to beat a steady supply of water power.

At Daniel Lord's 1850 dam near School Street, however, a newer technology is at work. In a small, leased annex to the Benjamin & Allen Agricultural Works, a foundry and machine shop, water power not only drives belts for machinery, but turns the 22.5-kilovolt electric generator that comprises the entire power capability of the Oakland Electric Light Company, organized in 1887 and led by president Orestes Crowell.

For $600 a year, the company lights the streets of Oakland from dusk to 10 PM — except on moonlit nights, frugal local officials had provided in the contract. With the street-lighting contract and other power users, the little electric company serves about 100 customers.[3]

Fort Halifax switch board, 1913

Gear for 'isolated plants'

← Power house at Page's Mill

Who were Wyman and Eaton?

The partners who bought the Oakland Electric Light Company in 1899 were both Maine men, but not peas in a pod.

The younger, stockier man, Walter Scott Wyman, was a former engineering student working as telegrapher and manager of the Waterville & Fairfield Railway and Electric Company. The older, taller, leaner Harvey Doane Eaton was a Waterville attorney.

Wyman was a local boy, born in Oakland (known as West Waterville until 1883) on May 6, 1874. His father, Hiram Wyman, worked at the Dunn Edge Tool Company, an axe- and scythe-making establishment downstream a ways from the Benjamin & Allen mill. Walter Wyman attended local schools and the Coburn Classical Institute in Waterville, then spent three years at Tufts College, where his varied courses included electrical engineering, geometry, machine drawing, rhetoric, and "vise and machine work." He worked at a campus store, and had summer jobs at the Bar Harbor telegraph office of Western Union and as station operator at the Oakland Electric Light Company. His first job after leaving college was as inspector and assistant superintendent of the Maine Water Company in Waterville, but he soon moved to the staff of the Waterville and Fairfield Railway and Light Company. He was, in other words, well acquainted with electricity, water power, and business operations.[a]

Eaton was born in North Cornville, farming country, on September 20, 1862. After attending local grammar school, he studied at Somerset Classical Academy in nearby Athens, then at Coburn Classical Institute. Eaton graduated from Colby College in 1887, then took a law degree from Harvard University in 1891, whereupon he returned to Waterville and opened a law office.[b]

The two met sometime in the early 1890s. Wyman's electrical and business background and Eaton's training in law and financial acumen laid the foundation for a productive partnership when opportunity arose on the banks of the Messalonskee Stream.Eaton was the first president of the Oakland Electric Company after the 1899 purchase, then Messalonskee Electric, then Central Maine Power. He stepped down in 1924, apparently objecting to the pending sale of CMP to the Middle West Utilities holding company, and returned to the practice of law and the pursuit of civic betterments.

In his civic life, Eaton drafted a charter and helped win legislative and voter approval in 1899 for the Kennebec Water District, the first municipal water district in Maine. While working up his plans in this pre-Oakland Electric phase, Eaton consulted with Wyman on engineering and water-source issues.[c] A private water company had been serving Waterville and Fairfield from the polluted end of the Messalonskee Stream; when the district began operating in 1905, it drew fresh water from China Lake. Eaton served as the district's general counsel into his eighties. Upon his death on October 17, 1953, a columnist for the Waterville *Morning Sentinel* wrote, "To this reporter, the establishment of the Kennebec Water District was a more important accomplishment than the start of the Central Maine Power Company, with which he also was identified. Attorney Eaton didn't become a millionaire from either endeavor. He served other people and he served well."[d]

Wyman succeeded Eaton as president of CMP in 1924, and presided over the financing and execution of a major expansion of Maine's hydroelectric capacity. He died of heart disease at his Augusta home on November 15, 1942. He had been working from his sickbed on completing the acquisition of Cumberland County Light & Power Company.

When Wyman died, Harvey Eaton told the press, "For simple courage, clear foresight, and sublime faith in the future we never had his equal in Maine... Our last meeting was at his house only a few days ago. Never were greeting and parting more warm and kindly. Goodbye, old friend."[e]

W.S. Wyman Station, Bingham →

Competitor lighting gas lamps →

Lineman Nathan Longfellow, 1906

This was nothing unusual. In the 1890s, the electric-power business was typically local and small-scale. Almost 2,000 local electric companies were providing power and light from central generating stations around the United States in 1891.[4] But many thousands of other generators were strictly on-site units, powering only lights or machinery in a single building or mill complex.

The small producers reflected both the infancy of the industry and the limits of technology. It was news in 1896 when a Niagara Falls, N.Y., power plant designed by George Westinghouse moved electricity via alternating currents to power lights and trolleys in Buffalo, 20 miles away. The direct-current technology favored by Thomas Edison generally limited power transfer to a half-mile radius from the power plant; unlike AC, direct current couldn't be boosted to offset line resistance.[5]

George Westinghouse, alternating-current champion (Corbis/Bettmann)

Dozens of Maine communities had one or more local gas-light or electric companies in the 1890s: Augusta, Bangor, Bath, Biddeford, Brunswick, Camden, Gardiner, Hallowell, Portland, Rockland, Saco, Waterville, and others. Only a year after Edison's Pearl Street Station began small-scale power distribution in New York City, the New England Weston Illuminating Company was powering 100 arc lights in the Monument Square area of Portland, while the Consolidated Electric Light Company was operating a direct-current generator on Plum Street.[6]

The Oakland Electric Light Company was not the first, or the biggest, or the most modern electric company in Maine. But it was the birthplace of something bigger than any of the electric companies of its day.

Young Walter S. Wyman was local manager for the Waterville and Fairfield Railway and Light Company when word got out that the owners of Oakland electric plant might be willing to sell. Wyman and a local acquaintance, attorney Harvey D. Eaton, discussed the idea. Eaton arranged a loan and mortgaged some real estate to raise the $4,500 purchase price.

On November 7, 1899, Eaton recalled, "After the evening meal, Mr. Wyman and I hired a livery-stable team, drove the five miles to Oakland, met the owners of the plant, and traded with them. When we drove back to Waterville late that night, we both knew that we had started something, but neither of us was quite sure just where we might land."[7]

On December 26, they reorganized as the Oakland Electric Company with Eaton as president and Wyman as general manager. The firm had $10,000 in capital stock and authority to do business in Oakland and Belgrade. It was a part-time venture: Eaton kept practicing law, and Wyman stayed at his post in Waterville until the management told him he must choose between them and the Oakland venture. He talked to Eaton, then quit the railroad job.

In buying that small hydro-electric generator making light from the river, Eaton and Wyman launched an enterprise that would grow into Central Maine Power Company.

Harvey Eaton,
President 1899-1924

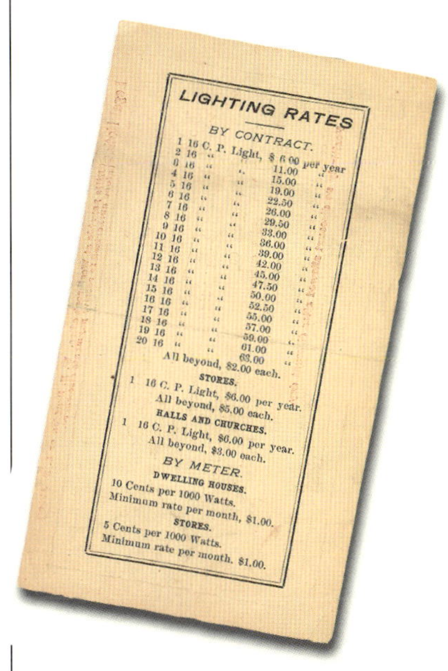

LIGHTING RATES

BY CONTRACT.

1	16 C. P. Light,	$ 6.00 per year
2	16 " "	11.00 "
3	16 " "	15.00 "
4	16 " "	19.00 "
5	16 " "	22.50 "
6	16 " "	26.00 "
7	16 " "	29.50 "
8	16 " "	33.00 "
9	16 " "	36.00 "
10	16 " "	39.00 "
11	16 " "	42.00 "
12	16 " "	45.00 "
13	16 " "	47.50 "
14	16 " "	50.00 "
15	16 " "	52.50 "
16	16 " "	55.00 "
17	16 " "	57.00 "
18	16 " "	59.00 "
19	16 " "	61.00 "
20	16 " "	63.00 "

All beyond, $2.00 each.

STORES.

1 16 C. P. Light, $6.00 per year.
All beyond, $5.00 each.

HALLS AND CHURCHES.

1 16 C. P. Light, $6.00 per year.
All beyond, $3.00 each.

BY METER.

DWELLING HOUSES.

10 Cents per 1000 Watts.
Minimum rate per month, $1.00.

STORES.

5 Cents per 1000 Watts.
Minimum rate per month. $1.00.

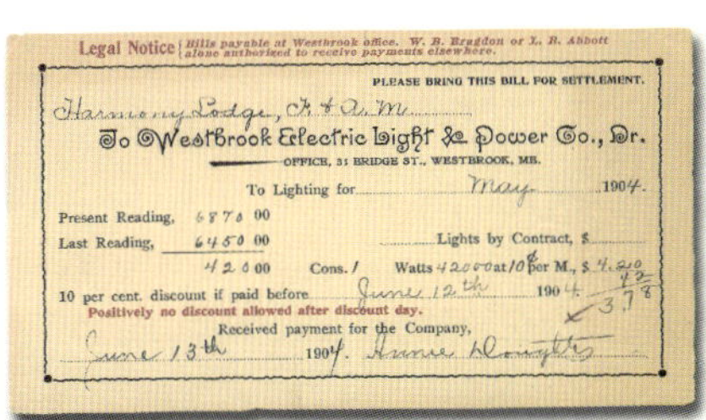

Legal Notice { Bills payable at Westbrook office. W. B. Bragdon or L. B. Abbott alone authorized to receive payments elsewhere.

PLEASE BRING THIS BILL FOR SETTLEMENT.

Harmony Lodge, F. & A. M.

To Westbrook Electric Light & Power Co., Dr.

OFFICE, 31 BRIDGE ST., WESTBROOK, ME.

To Lighting for May 1904.

Present Reading, 6870 00
Last Reading, 6450 00
420 00 Cons. / Watts 42000 at 10¢ per M., $ 4.20
Lights by Contract, $

10 per cent. discount if paid before June 12th 1904. 42 / 3.78

Positively no discount allowed after discount day.

Received payment for the Company,
June 13th 1904.

← Hydro gear for West Buxton, 1906

The Setting

Selling wind-up Victor gramophones

Electricity was not new at the turn of the century, but it was still uncommon.

By the mid-1870s, some streets in New York, Cleveland, London, Paris, and other cities had been lit by exposed-element electric arc lights. They were pole-mounted devices that operated like large, continuously igniting spark plugs. Although the Paris Opera used arc lights at an 1849 production, their light was generally thought too glaring and dangerous for indoor use.[8]

City lighting was more commonly supplied by piped gas, often made by heating coal to extract flammable vapors. Customers enjoyed the easily controllable light, but complained of the smell, stuffy air, sooty fabrics, and the risk of explosion. Alternatives, especially in the country, included kerosene and candles, with their own drawbacks.

In a rural state like Maine — in 1900, the U.S. Census recorded that fully 65 percent of its 914,000 inhabitants lived in communities of fewer than 2,500 people — life before electricity meant, among other things, quiet evenings. Historian David Nye comments:

> There was less light at night, and people tended to cluster around what little there was. The night outside was darker than the city's dark. The

← Overleaf: Electric lights and lines on the Pier, Old Orchard Beach

Wiring Hallowell, ca. 1890 →

> farmhouse had a lower noise level, and not just because there was no television; it had no humming refrigerator, no flushing toilet, no whirring appliance motors. Things did not make noises; the only sounds came from people, animals, and natural forces, like the wind.[9]

Widespread distribution of electric light and power became practicable after Edison's 1879 development of the enclosed incandescent light and after Nikola Tesla's 1888 patent for multi-phase alternating-current equipment. Edison had set up the world's first central-station (as opposed to on-site) power plant on Pearl Street in New York City in 1882. But the low-voltage, direct-current power limited the station's reach to a few blocks. So Edison picked his site to include customers like the *New York Times,* whose patronage would maximize publicity for the Edison light.

Electric plants sprang up wherever there was a demand for street lighting, power for trolley cars, and illumination for businesses. The year 1882 saw not only Edison's Pearl Street Station; but also, in Appleton, Wisconsin, the first hydroelectric power plant, and eight others. In Portland, Maine, the Consolidated Electric Light Company began building a system based on three steam-driven generators on Center Street. The number of U.S. power plants distributing electricity, as distinct from on-site generators serving the host property, jumped to 468 by 1889, and to 1,807 by 1899.[10]

← Power house, Forest Avenue, Portland, 1912

The horse yields to the electron

It is 1890. You are standing at Congress and Free streets, a busy corner in Maine's largest city, Portland.

The trolley stops, and you step forward to board it and ride to Monument Square.

Mind the horse droppings.

A state report of 1890 lists six "street railways" or trolley lines in what is now the CMP service area. Five of them use horses to pull the cars along the rails: the Portland Railway Company, the Lewiston and Auburn Horse Railroad, the Fryeburg Horse Railroad, the Biddeford and Saco Railroad, and the Waterville and Fairfield Horse Railroad.[f]

The sixth, the electric Augusta, Hallowell and Gardiner Railway, had just started operations in 1890. Its nine cars plied seven miles of track along the Kennebec. Lines were later extended to Winthrop and to an amusement park near the Old Soldiers Home at Togus.

Electrification of trolleys took off rapidly after the success of the pioneering electric-trolley system of Richmond, Virginia, in 1887. By 1890, about 200 American cities had built or ordered electric trolley systems.[g] The number included Portland, which began electric trolley runs in June 1891.

Horsecars had answered a real need: growing cities were too big to navigate on foot. But horsepower had its problems. The estimated 100,000 horses and mules pulling trolleys in 1880 were leaving a million pounds of manure on the streets every day, they increased the crowding and danger of the streets, and their hard working conditions upset many people.[h]

Enclosed cars for your trolleying comfort

Improved dynamos for power plants and motors for the trolley cars transformed the street railways, and provided a large, dependable load for electric companies: two-thirds of the electric load of Samuel Insull's Chicago utilities came from trolleys and elevated trains.

The business synergies of power and load led to many consolidations, such as the 1891 combination of the Waterville and Fairfield Railroad, the Waterville Electric Light and Power Company, and the Fairfield Electric Company into the Waterville and Fairfield Railway and Light Company — the future, temporary employer of Walter Wyman.

The costs of building and operating trolleys demanded high-volume ridership: an empty car cost nearly as much to run as a packed car. In the days before auto ownership was common, trolley companies could draw vitally needed riders by extending track to or even building attractions. In 1914, the Rockland, Thomaston and Camden Street Railway carried riders to the 72-acre Oakland Park a few miles out of Rockland, where people could enjoy the seashore, a restaurant, amusements, and a dance hall. The Cape Cottage Casino in Cape Elizabeth, Riverton Park on the Portland-Westbrook line, and Casco Castle in South Freeport were also popular destinations for trolley riders.

Electric-trolley operations grew and combined into larger enterprises for more than 30 years. A direct route between Lewiston and Portland, for example, began service in June 1914, with nine cars bearing Azalea, Clematis, Narcissus, and other floral names. Between the terminals, waiting rooms were built at West Falmouth, Gray, and Danville. The 90-minute trip had 11 stops and cost 75 cents. The Portland-Lewiston Interurban became part of the Androscoggin Electric Company, which was absorbed into CMP in 1920.

Trolleys went into a general decline after 1920 as costs and regulation increased, and as gasoline-powered autos and buses offered consumers new and convenient choices. After folding several smaller lines, CMP exited the inter-urban trolley business on June 29, 1933, with a final Portland-Lewiston transit by the trolley Arbutus, which had made the line's first run 19 years earlier. The Waterville trolley operation, CMP's last, was abandoned in 1937.

CMP, which had replaced its Thomaston-Warren trolley with a bus in 1925, acquired another bus line in 1942 with its acquisition of the Cumberland County electric utility. CMP sold the 88-bus fleet in December 1944. By that time, Maine's electric trolleys, like the horse-drawn trolleys before them, were museum pieces.

Trolley tracks and wires, Congress Street, Portland,ca. 1900

Street lighting, then trolleys, then factories was the usual sequence of customer targeting for early electric companies. The costs of constructing a system needed to be spread over a large, stable base of demand, preferably one reached with a minimum of line construction. The dispersion of the residential market made home lighting initially unappealing to electric companies, while costs of service limited the appeal to ordinary citizens. One historian notes, "In the 1880s, [electric lighting] was a luxury item of conspicuous consumption; one bulb alone cost half a day's common wages, or one dollar, and a kilowatt-hour of current cost as much as twenty cents."[11] The 24 cents paid by customers of Edison's Pearl Street Station in 1882 was the equivalent of roughly $3.50 per kilowatt-hour in 1998 purchasing power.[12]

Even as late as 1897, the average price for a kilowatt-hour of electricity was about 10 cents. When a standard loaf of bread cost three cents and first-class

All aboard: Augusta, bound for Winthrop, ca. 1900 →

postage cost two cents, electricity was not yet a household bargain. For most electric companies, serious pursuit of the residential market therefore didn't start until about 1910, when the average cost of electricity had declined to a more attractive 2.5 cents per kilowatt-hour. [13]

These considerations were common, and they figured into Wyman and Eaton's business calculations. But to Wyman's engineering eye, Maine's river systems offered a golden opportunity to support a network of power plants that could deliver economical energy to customers at some distance from the power plants. His vision, stated in an early bulletin to employees, was to "make possible the furnishing of electricity in any quantity from a four candle-power lamp to a 1,000-horsepower motor anywhere in the territory covered by our lines." [14]

Eaton and Wyman had a company. They had a vision. They went to work.

The Takeoff

Oakland was a busy little town, but building an interconnected electric system to develop Maine's huge river resources required that Wyman and Eaton expand their business.

Line crew, North Gorham, 1908

The first step was extending their lines to the Waterville city limit in 1900. There they interconnected to buy wholesale energy from the new Union Gas and Electric Company plant, also on the Messalonskee Stream. They shut down the little 22.5-kilowatt generator in the Benjamin & Allen mill.

The year 1901 complicated their lives. The Waterville and Fairfield Railway and Electric Company bought out Union Gas and Electric, the new power source for Oakland. Eaton made a bet on the future by buying several acres around the Rice's Rips rapids on the Messalonskee, for later development. Most of the $23,500 purchase was financed with a $16,500 loan from Peoples National Bank of Waterville. The deal was negotiated in Eaton's law office, with Eaton doing most of the talking — "Mr. Wyman was never a spokesman except when answering questions about the electrical business," Eaton said, "and then he had few equals."[15] The bank officers agreed to the loan, Eaton said, partly because a set of poorly behaving false teeth made it difficult for the only opponent to say much. The land was secured for future use, though construction did not begin until 1918.

← Overleaf: Dam builders at work, Fort Halifax, 1907

Motorman Joe Gillis and Conductor W.A. McAuly with customers, Waterville, ca. 1905 →

Union Gas & Electric Co. plant, Waterville

Meanwhile, the Waterville and Fairfield electric company's street-lighting contract with the City of Waterville was expiring in October 1901. The company had raised its rates after absorbing Union Gas and Electric, so Wyman and Eaton thought the city might be receptive to a new offer. But Oakland Electric had no charter to conduct business in Waterville, so Eaton presented an offer from "the more or less mythical Messalonskee Electric Company," with Wyman and Eaton acting in a co-partnership as individuals selling electricity.[16] Their offer included a promotional touch — two years' free lighting for the new Waterville City Hall to be dedicated in 1902.

Messalonskee Electric got the Waterville contract, even though the "more or less mythical" bidder had no power plant at the time, or even lines into Waterville. The partners set to work, buying a new generator to install in Oakland's Dunn Edge Tool Company, and installing more poles and lines to connect to the Waterville street-lighting system. This ended the brief period of serving electric customers while owning no power plants — a circumstance that would wait 98 years to be repeated, when CMP sold its power plants under a state mandate. Starting in January 1903, subscriptions for commercial and other private lighting were accepted, ensuring additional revenues for the new operation.

George Hegarty, early Wyman aide and early CMP chronicler

Setting a pole, Portland, ca. 1910 →

Some people doubted the business would last. Early in 1903, George D. Hegarty quit his job at the Maine Central Railroad to become Wyman's stenographer. When the railroad's general manager learned that Hegarty had quit, "he came to Waterville to see me, and, for something over a half hour, he tried to impress upon me why I should stay with the Maine Central Railroad, stating that I was going with two fellows who had no money and no backing and they could not possibly succeed."[17] That was not an unreasonable view: in the years ahead, Hegarty saw first-hand the bitter competition with the Waterville and Fairfield operation in open commerce, and in quiet lobbying at City Hall and the Legislature.

PLEASE BRING THIS BILL WITH YOU

H A BICKNELL

109 SPRING ST
GARDINER ME

JULY 31
1919 109

To Central Maine Power Company, Dr.

To Bills Rendered for Electric Current
(NO DISCOUNT ALLOWED ON ABOVE ITEM)

Present Reading 282

Previous " 270

K.W.H. used, 12 @ .09 — 1.08

Less Discount

% Discount if paid at our office on or before the 15th of the following month.

Received Payment for the Company,

191

NO DISCOUNT ALLOWED AFTER 15TH OF MONTH
PLEASE NOT ASK FOR IT

MINIMUM MONTHLY CHARGE, 75c.

THIS BILL IS SUBJECT TO ALL CONTRACT CONDITIONS

After an initial rebuff in 1903, the Messalonskee Electric Company was formally chartered by the Maine Legislature in 1905, with authority to serve Oakland, Waterville, Fairfield, Benton, and Winslow. After the organizational meeting of July 25, 1905, the Oakland Electric Company was no more. More important, from Wyman's point of view, drawing a number of communities into an authorized service area offered the opportunity to improve reliability and reduce costs by connecting electrical systems and building larger generating units. "It was simply impossible," Eaton said of his partner, "to keep up with his knowledge and understanding of the needs for expansion."[18]

← Admiring new electric refrigerators at a CMP appliance store

George Hegarty knew from personal experience what Wyman's expansion plans entailed: long days, Sunday rides reconnoitering potential hydro sites, and frequent visits to factory owners who might take power, suppliers who might provide materials and equipment, bankers who might advance credit, and power plants that might be acquired. Hegarty didn't complain, for Wyman "never asked anyone to do anything that he was not doing himself and, with small earnings, it was quite some time before he could employ a sufficient number of people to handle the work within [normal] hour limitations." [19]

Expansion continued, aided by Messalonskee Electric's offer of a minimal $1 per month residential-service plan. Perhaps new home-owners or apartment-dwellers would install only one outlet in the kitchen ceiling for sparing use of a light bulb or a new electric iron. But once the wires were in and the convenience of electricity was apparent, more business would follow. The demand was there from homes, stores, and "manufactories." A 1909 preferred-stock prospectus noted, "The business in Waterville and vicinity is rapidly growing and new prospects are coming faster than the current can be provided to supply them," with 210 new service drops in 1908 and 107 in the first half of 1909. [20]

Competition for the ice companies

Installing hydro gear, Fort Halifax →

Still, large accounts to justify larger, more efficient generating plants were the key to reducing unit costs and promoting long-term growth. Wyman and Eaton had bought several parcels of land along the Sebasticook River in Winslow to secure another future hydro site. They were soon able to make use of it. Signing a 30-year contract with backers of a new street railway, they used a funding advance to build the Fort Halifax power plant on the Sebasticook. The plant was completed in 1907, and in mid-1908 began powering the Waterville, Augusta, and Lewiston interurban railway, providing more than $30,000 a year in electric revenues — almost half Messalonskee's total revenues. Another big victory was the 1909 contract, which required special legislation, to supply 750 kilowatts of power to the Edwards Manufacturing Company in Augusta, with more for lighting and emergency service.

Bill Cilley, mobile meter tester, North Dexter, 1926

The assets of Messalonskee Electric and its Fort Halifax Power Company were then mortgaged as security for $5 million in bonds, and another $2 million was raised through a sale of common stock — though Wyman and Eaton still had a majority owners' interest. Deploying their new capital, Wyman and Eaton formed the Robinson Land Company to acquire additional property in

Bingham and Moscow for hydro development (an idea still 20 years from fruition); bought the Kennebec Light and Heat Company that served Augusta, Hallowell, and Gardiner; and constructed a new, 7,500-kilowatt coal-fired power station in Farmingdale. In less than a decade, the partners had progressed from scraping up $4,500 for a tiny generator, to raising millions to buy entire companies and build new power plants.

The State of Maine cooperated in the expansion. A 1907 law allowed Messalonskee Electric to buy capital stock in other electric utilities. Another law in 1909 broadened that power, authorizing stock purchases in any Maine corporation. [21]

Not every development in this period pleased the partners. Many Maine people looked with alarm at the increasing private development of water power. The Union Water-Power Company, later to become part of CMP, stirred up controversy in 1907 and was defeated in its attempt to draw down Rangeley Lake. [22] Part of the public concern was that hydro developers might sign contracts to export this economical power, leaving rural areas far behind in development and standards of living. Another concern was that new businesses might not locate in Maine if they could stay near New England's urban centers and still enjoy cheap power from Maine rivers.

Farmingdale Steam Plant

Augusta store decked out for Christmas, 1925

Marketing the marvels

Incandescent lighting might be a marvel in itself, but there were plenty of others awaiting new electric customers in the early years of the 20th century: electric irons, electric sewing machines, electric stoves, electric refrigerators, electric toasters, electric vacuum cleaners, electric washers. The potential market was large: only one in 10 American homes had electricity in 1910, and lighting was still the major use of electricity.[i]

Starting in 1916, CMP appliance stores invited wonder and courted desire with bright window displays and well-stocked showrooms. In Augusta, Brunswick, Dexter, Greenville, Rockland, Union, and other towns, salespeople demonstrated and persuaded. The stores generated revenue themselves, plus demand for more electricity, upgraded wiring, and — as a 1920 *Exciter* cartoon showed — dual-outlet adapters so the housewife could iron electrically without having to unscrew her electric bulb.

The stores competed for sales honors and prizes. The 1925 "Eat More Toast" campaign aimed to beat the prior year's record of 500 Universal toasters sold. If the ads, mailers, and placards don't draw the customer, one bit of sales advice said, invite Mrs. Jones into the store a free cup of coffee from the electric percolator, then show her how she can control the temperature while cooking biscuits electrically, eliminate toting wood or coal, and forget cleaning up ashes. Selling appliances was "an object with a high purpose — for every electrical appliance saves somebody steps, increases somebody's comfort, or contributes something to health and happiness."[j]

The selling wasn't confined to stores. In Rockland on May 23, 1926, more than 800 people toured CMP securities-sales manager Lincoln McRae's specially wired home at 223 Broadway with "mingled comments of surprise and wonderment." No ceiling outlets

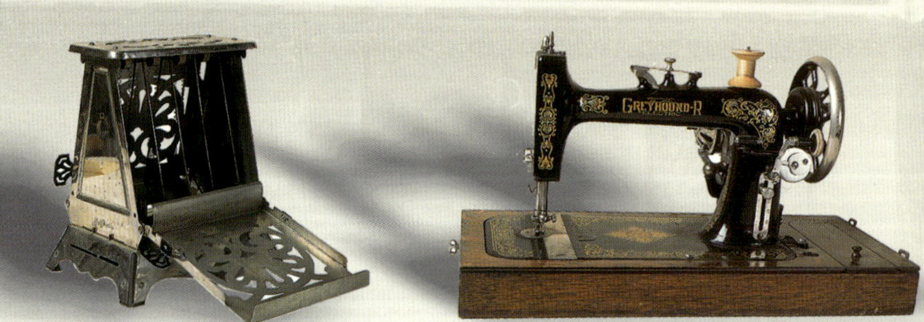

marred the gentility of the living room: concealed wires fed wall outlets. The service connection to the house ran underground. An electric fan in the kitchen wall vented cooking odors. Closet lights came on automatically when the door was opened.[k] Considering that the White House had changed from blocks of ice to electricity to refrigerate President Calvin Coolidge's eggs and milk only two years before, these were indeed marvelous touches.

Farmers lucky enough to live near electric-distribution lines — nationally, 90 percent did not as late as 1920 — were shown the wonders of electric milkers and electric milk coolers, not to mention the electric silage cutter and the electric sausage stuffer. Commercial customers weren't overlooked, either. A year-long sales campaign electrified 11 bakeries in CMP's service area by early 1925, including a 30-ton electric oven at Lepage's Bakery in Lewiston that could turn out 1,700 loaves, 150 pies, and 400 dozen other baked goods daily. Some proud innovators updated their names: Belfast was home to the Curtis Electric Bakery, while Pittsfield boasted Wright's Electric Bakery.[l]

Personal computers, microwave ovens, televisions, videocassette players, compact-disc players, electric hedge clippers, and other baubles were still far off. But even in the 1920s, with electric radios and electric phonographs added to the early mix of electric appliances, there were still plenty of electric marvels to sell.

Concern crystallized into a proposed law to ban hydro-power exports. Wyman thought this was foolish. On March 11, 1909, he wrote to an Island Falls resident, encouraging him to make his voice heard in the Legislature and plying him with arguments:

> We feel as though power is the principal resource that Maine has outside of lumber and that in the future, the development and sale of the power which is now running to waste, amounting to nearly one and a half million Horse Power, was going to be one of the great industries of the State.... While the lighting business has formed a large part of the electric business in the past, it is rapidly becoming a comparatively small portion of the total business done.... We want to see Maine grow and we do not want to see restrictions imposed which will prevent that growth and discourage capital from investing in our natural resources.[23]

The SURPLUS POWER EXPORT LAW

ISSUED BY CENTRAL MAINE POWER CO.
W. S. WYMAN, PRESIDENT
W. B. SKELTON, VICE PRESIDENT

Wyman could marshall many arguments: The greatest barrier to electrifying rural Maine was not a possible shortage of power, but the high cost of installing power lines in sparsely populated areas versus their modest expected revenues — a business problem that would exist whether power were exported or not. No other state had seen reason to ban power exports. Further, Wyman believed, few industries were so sensitive to power costs that they would be

The SURPLUS POWER EXPORT LAW

1. WATER POWER IN MAINE—ITS EXTENT AND USE

It is possible to develop on the principal Maine rivers and their tributaries about 1,600,000 horse-power, which would produce in the average year about 7,000,000,000 kilowatt hours of useful power. About 600,000 horsepower has already been developed, and this produces about 2,600,000,000 kilowatt hours in the average year.

That is, the rivers in Maine are doing about one-third the work they are capable of doing. The balance of their power runs to waste.

Maine's present policy, which prohibits the export of any surplus power, not only prevents the most efficient use of the developed water power within the State, but seriously delays the time when the water powers which are not developed at all and are going to waste will begin to do useful work.

The Androscoggin is the most highly developed of the larger Maine rivers; the Penobscot, the Kennebec and the Saco following in order. In spite of its development, however, the Androscoggin is still capable of producing more than twice as much useful power as it now produces. The other rivers could produce several times as much power as they now produce.

[3]

Horse fountain defying power lines, Maine Street, Brunswick, 1907 →

Hydro construction, West Buxton, 1906

induced to move to Maine by a ban on power exports. And exports could be redirected to in-state use as soon as rising demand cut into the surplus available for export. Worst of all, reducing the scale of power projects to match Maine's demand only would sacrifice the scale economies possible in bigger projects, thereby delaying price cuts and retarding economic growth.[24]

Pole crew, Portland, ca. 1915

But Messalonskee Electric's opposition could not prevent the popular concern from becoming a legal prohibition. With state Senator, later Governor, Percival Baxter leading the export-ban forces, the Maine Legislature in 1909 enacted "the Fernald Law," named for Governor Bert Fernald.

The Fernald Law annoyed Wyman for decades, and he continued to speak against it. Fifteen years of the ban had not persuaded new industry to move to Maine, he noted, while it had prevented early development of larger hydro projects with lower unit costs. In a signed 1925 ad placed in several Maine newspapers, Wyman said "This law should be modified or repealed so as to permit surplus power to be exported."[25]

Line truck ready for action, 1914

A proposed law allowing the export of "surplus or waste water power only" was sent out to referendum in 1929, but voters rejected it, 53,000 to 7,000.[26] At that point, Wyman stopped campaigning: "The people have built us up and I do not intend to run contrary to their wishes."[27] The Fernald Law was not repealed until 1955, more than a decade after Wyman's death, finally enabling Maine to benefit from electrical interconnection with the rest of New England.

Another challenge to Wyman's plans in the early 1920s came from the maverick Republican Percival Baxter, now governor. In 1923, Baxter blocked CMP's plans to develop the Dead River, arguing that the abutting public lands required state ownership and control of new reservoirs. CMP did not win the right to develop the site until 1927, but even then it was obliged to lease the public lands.[28]

Wyman did not object, however, to another assertion of state authority: Maine's establishment of a Public Utilities Commission. The Legislature created the PUC by statute; citizens ratified it by referendum. The Maine PUC began operations on December 1, 1914. One of the original three commissioners of the PUC was William B. Skelton, who later became chairman of CMP. Wisconsin and New York introduced state regulation of electric-company prices in 1907; 43 other states followed by 1914.[29] State regulation typically involved assigning exclusive retail "franchise" areas, and approving rates or "tariffs" designed to recover operating expenses plus a rate of return on stockholders' investment.

Union Falls power house, Saco River

Regulation offered some advantages for electric companies. They needed to raise lots of money up-front to build power plants and lines, but could then be threatened by a competitor whose bigger, newer plant had lower unit costs. Vicious price wars could break out in contested areas, leaving the loser unable to cover its interest costs and ruining its shareholders and bondholders. Regulation limited competition and gave the utility a legal right to rates that should cover its capital and operating costs. And in pre-Securities and Exchange Commission era of loosely constrained financial statements, any regulatory scrutiny of utility books was a security-marketing plus for companies that regularly required new capital. Employees selling CMP preferred stock in 1920 were urged to point to "consistently growing demand" for electricity and note that "Competition is regulated by the Public Utilities Commission." So, they could then ask their prospects, "Could anything be safer or surer?"[30]

Henry Provost (by axe handle) and friends, 1926

In return for an exclusive franchise and reasonable assurance of covering capital costs, however, utilities had to serve any customer who wanted electricity, and ensure a safe, adequate, and economical supply of power.[31] This required long-term demand projections, financing programs, and construction planning — obligations of great consequence in the decades to come.

Linemens' gear

After 1909, with more than 4,500 customers, Wyman and Eaton launched their second decade of operations with a name change. As George Hegarty said, "It seemed advisable — in fact, the bankers said people could not pronounce 'Messalonskee' — to have a more significant and distinguishing name."[32] On January 25, 1910, the shareholders of Messalonskee Electric changed the name to Central Maine Power Company, still with Eaton as president and Wyman as general manager.

Growth required a new headquarters. The company's main office had been in Waterville for several years, in a former stable at 12 Charles Street. Early in 1912, it moved to the former Kennebec Light and Heat building at 313 Water Street, Augusta. Although moved two more times — to 9 Green Street in 1927, and to 83 Edison Drive in 1976 — CMP's main office has been in Augusta ever since. Augusta was also chosen for the first CMP electric-appliance store, opened in 1916.

Growth also continued through acquisitions. Between 1910 and the U.S. entry into World War I in 1917, CMP bought electric companies in Bingham,

Dexter, Skowhegan, Vassalboro, Clinton, Corinna, Richmond, and Waterville — where, in 1911, CMP bought out its main rival, the Waterville and Fairfield Railway and Light Company, which in the meantime had recaptured the city's street-lighting contract. Federal-government urging led to rapid development of the Rice's Rips hydro site and high-voltage extensions to the shipyard at Bath. Meanwhile, other power plants had been put into service at Dennistown, Fairfield, Oakland, Belfast, and Limerick.

Cumberland County Power & Light outing, 1920

By 1919, the electric-customer count had exploded to 21,361 and the CMP system boasted 22,000 kilowatts of capacity — almost a thousand times the power of the original generator in the Benjamin & Allen Agricultural Works. Wyman, Eaton, and a few others still controlled the capital stock, but nearly 2,400 other people had purchased shares of CMP 6% and 7% preferred stock. Agents and CMP employees touted the preferred stock, competing for prizes and commissions.

For the Christmas bonus in 1900, Harvey Eaton noted, "Two $5 gold pieces sufficed for the entire crew."[33] Now, going on 20 years later, CMP had achieved takeoff.

← Electric conveniences on display

The Boom

Solve problem, build sales, 1920

The 1920s were boom years for most Americans. For CMP, the themes of these high-growth times were Maine water and Middle West Utilities.

Wyman led CMP into the cash-laden arms of Samuel Insull's vast Middle West Utilities holding company, then used Insull's great resources to bankroll major development of Maine's water-power resources.

Buying local electric companies, extending lines, and developing new power sources required repeated rounds of financing. There were limits to bank loans and sales of preferred stock through employee sales drives. On the other hand, Wyman and Eaton had resisted lenders' suggestions that they and other equity holders sell off some of their owners' stake in the company.

So CMP faced a financing challenge. Most of the preferred stock required a 7 percent dividend, and a 1921 offer of $3 million in 7 percent mortgage bonds had to be sold at a 10 percent discount, raising the effective cost of the money. Meanwhile, the 1920 purchase of the Androscoggin Electric Company had consumed more funds, and meeting the growing demands of the Lewiston-Auburn area would require additional infrastructure investment. Three pending river projects — hydro-electric dams at Bingham and Lewiston, and a storage dam on the Dead River — would require $20 million, a huge sum for the time that could not be raised through CMP's accustomed methods.[34]

Transmission-line builders, near Madison, 1920s →

← Overleaf: Electric trolleys on Monument Square, Portland, ca. 1917

As these challenges mounted, the Eaton-Wyman partnership broke up — though each man continued to speak well of the other. Harvey Eaton resigned as president of CMP effective January 29, 1924, being immediately succeeded by Wyman. He resumed his practice of law in Waterville and served on the CMP board until August 3, 1925, when some new members arrived after a major change pushed by Wyman.

Walter Wyman,
President 1924-1942

The Insulls, Edison protégé Samuel and his brother Martin, were looking around New England. Wyman and his advisers talked with them.

On June 26, 1925, Wyman told CMP employees through a letter in the *Exciter* that Middle West was offering $140 for each share of CMP's common stock, which was closely held, but had been traded privately for $40 a share prior to the Insull offer.[35] Meanwhile, CMP employees and other Mainers totaling more than 12,000 people had bought over $10 million of the publicly offered, fixed-dividend CMP preferred stock. For their benefit Wyman noted that "The preferred shareholders in companies bought by [the Insulls] have materially benefited from their control." Further, Middle West's policy was to retain existing management in acquired operating companies, so "Our stockholders may rest assured that Central Maine Power Company will continue to operate under Maine officials and that its policy will be for Maine's best interests."

Who was Samuel Insull?

Samuel Insull "is one of the great captains of industry of America," the CMP *Exciter* pronounced on July 31, 1925, and his Middle West Utilities organization is "one of the great electrical holding companies of the world."

The effusion wasn't just in-house puffery for the man who had bought out CMP. Insull was widely regarded as a genius at building up utilities, using new efficiencies to reduce rates, then using the new demand to build some more. He also had a genius for intricate financial moves, but that wasn't widely appreciated until the Roaring '20s had passed into the Depression of the 1930s.

Born in London in 1859, Insull was hired as stenographer to Thomas Edison's chief of European operations. Adding bookkeeping and finance to his skills, Insull rose quickly and moved to New York as Edison's assistant as preparations were under way to open the Pearl Street Station in 1882. Insull scouted out new locations for Edison's favored direct-current generators, and developed a manufacturing facility in Schenectady, New York, that was the start of the General Electric Company.[m]

When Edison sold his manufacturing operation in 1892, Insull moved to take charge of the Chicago Edison Company. The utility faced stiff competition from the Chicago Arc Light Company, 18 smaller utilities, and about 500 on-site generators. Taking advantage of an 1893 financial panic, Insull bought Chicago Arc Light and other nearby utilities, and started work on large new power plants, aiming for organizational and generating efficiencies that would permit lower rates. He further sharpened his competitive position by developing devices that would allow direct- and alternating-current systems to work together, by making use of a new meter that measured level of demand as well as usage to encourage spreading load to off-peak hours, and by cultivating sales to trolley lines and the elevated railways so their early- and late-day loads would let his plants spend more time at higher levels of output. His efforts helped drive average electric rates in Chicago from 19.5 cents per

kilowatt-hour in 1898 to 8 cents in 1911.[n] (Even this dramatic decrease left household electricity a comparative luxury: 8 cents in 1911 was the equivalent of about $1.25 in 1998 purchasing power, whereas CMP's average residential kilowatt-hour in 1998 actually sold for 13 cents.)

In 1912, Insull took his empire-building to an entirely new level by forming Middle West Utilities. MWU grew into a five-layered holding company, with each layer's units holding the stock of the companies in the layer below. Asset values were inflated before purchases by stage-managed trades, and propped up afterwards by artificially low depreciation rates so they could back more issuances of debt. Income was padded by paying dividends to upstream companies out of invested capital rather than out of real earnings. It was a financial pyramid that would last only as long as eager investors kept it growing with new stock purchases.

Meanwhile, Insull's great resources let him buy nearly anything. "In 1925," a business historian reports, "he bought out a utility executive who controlled a large block of generating capacity and was proud of his independence. Asked why he had sold out, the man replied, 'What in the hell would you do if someone came along and offered you three times as much as your company was ever worth?'"[o]

By 1932, MWU and seven other interstate holding companies controlled three-quarters of the investor-owned utilities in America.[p] State regulation — which Insull had championed as early as 1898 — touched only the operating companies, not the upstream, cross-boundary layers, and few regulations restricted chicanery in finance or ingenuity in financial reporting.

At its height, Middle West Utilities operated in 19 states ranging from Maine to Texas to North Dakota. Other Insull companies operated in a dozen more, extending his lines of business across electricity, gas, water, trolley, and ice companies.[q] But MWU began to unravel after the stock-market crash of 1929 and major bank failures in 1931-32. Most operating utilities, including CMP, pulled through the Depression, but the holding-company tent was stretched too thin. Unable to cover his interest costs or to obtain credit, Insull put MWU into receivership at a loss of more than $800 million. Other Insull organizations collapsed as well, forcing him to resign from more than 60 chairmanships and presidencies. More than 275,000 MWU shareholders and 160,000 bondholders lost their money.

Indicted by Illinois for embezzlement and larceny in 1932, Insull fled to Greece, was expelled, fled to Turkey, and was extradited. He survived the state trial and two federal trials, then moved to Paris, where he died in 1938. By that time, the creation of the federal Securities and Exchange Commission and the Public Utilities Holding Company Act of 1935 — limiting corporate layers, restricting geographic reach, and imposing strict financial-reporting requirements — started the breakup of hundreds of holding companies to make an encore of the Middle West Utilities drama impossible.

Led off to jail, Chicago, 1934
(Corbis/Hulton-Deutsch Collection)

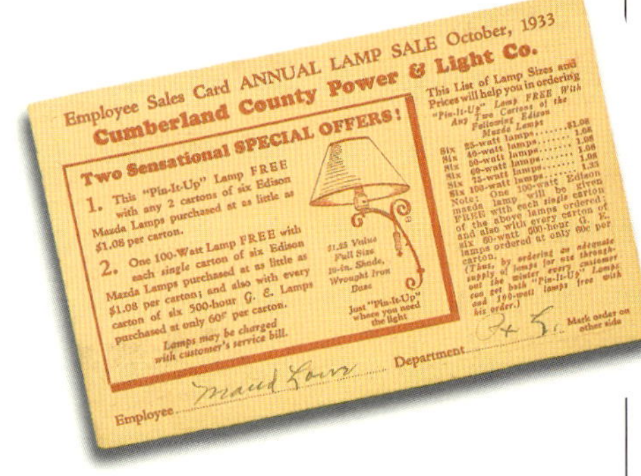

Employee Sales Card ANNUAL LAMP SALE October, 1933

Cumberland County Power & Light Co.

Two Sensational SPECIAL OFFERS!

1. This "Pin-It-Up" Lamp FREE with any 2 cartons of six Edison Mazda Lamps purchased at as little as $1.08 per carton.

2. One 100-Watt Lamp FREE with each *single* carton of six Edison Mazda Lamps purchased at as little as $1.08 per carton; and also with every carton of six 500-hour G. E. Lamps purchased at only 60¢ per carton.

Lamps may be charged with customer's service bill.

$1.25 Value Full Size 10-in. Shade, Wrought Iron Base

Just "Pin-It-Up" where you need the light

This List of Lamp Sizes and Prices will help you in ordering "Pin-It-Up" Lamp FREE With Any Two Cartons of the Following Edison Mazda Lamps

Six	25-watt lamps	$1.08
Six	40-watt lamps	1.08
Six	50-watt lamps	1.08
Six	60-watt lamps	1.08
Six	75-watt lamps	1.35

Six 100-watt Edison lamps. Note: One 100-watt Edison mazda lamp will be given FREE with each *single* carton of the above lamps ordered; and also with every carton of six 60-watt 500-hour G. E. lamps ordered at only 60¢ per carton.

(Thus, by ordering an adequate supply of lamps for use throughout the winter every customer can get both "Pin-It-Up" Lamps and 100-watt lamps free with his order.)

Mark order on other side

Employee .... Department ....

The sale was completed and approved "almost unanimously" by the common-stock owners.[36] Changes started at the top. The board of directors was reduced from 15 members to nine as of August 3, 1925. Eaton was gone, along with other veteran members including Wyman's scribe George Hegarty[37] and newspaper publisher Guy P. Gannett. Martin Insull moved onto the board as chairman, joined by two Insull colleagues from Chicago; Wyman and five other CMP veterans including former PUC commissioner William Skelton held the remaining seats.

So by way of the Middle West Utilities System, CMP moved into "The Insull Empire."

Middle West was itself only a part of Insull's holdings, but it owned 14 utility companies in New England, the Mid-Atlantic, the South, the Midwest, the Southwest, and the Northern Plains.

One of MWU's 14 constituent companies was the National Electric Power Company. This company in turn owned Michigan Electric Power, National Public Service, Ohio Electric Power, Pennsylvania Central Light and Power, and New England Public Service.

Chairman Martin Insull, hands clasped,with CMP managers, Augusta, ca. 1930

The layers continued. New England Public Service Company, led by Wyman, in turn owned Central Maine Power, Cumberland County Power and Light, Central Vermont Public Service, Public Service of New Hampshire, and National Light Heat and Power — which in turn owned Twin State Gas and Electric.[38]

CENTRAL MAINE POWER COMPANY

SPECIAL for APRIL and MAY

Special Prices on all orders received for electric wiring during the months of April and May, 1912, with one month's free lighting.

$27.00	$37.00	$42.00
6 rooms and front hall, with 1 two-light and 1 three-light fixture, balance drop lights, complete with shades, carbon lamps, key sockets, etc.	6 rooms and front hall, with 1 two-light, 1 three-light and 1 hall fixture, balance drop lights, complete with shades, Mazda lamps, chain pull sockets, etc.	6 rooms and front hall, with 1 two-light, 1 three-light and 1 hall fixture, balance drop lights, complete with shades, Mazda lamps, chain pull sockets, etc. With cellar or piazza light on switch.

We will wire your home complete as per above schedules, if the order is received during the months of April and May, 1912. The wiring will be concealed wherever possible and all material and workmanship guaranteed to be in accordance with the N. E. Insurance rules. Any of the above outfits will please you and they are at a price 20 per cent. less than the regular prices for such work.

There are hundreds of homes in this vicinity without electric lights. You should have the comfort and convenience afforded by modern methods of illumination. Call at our store. See our line of fixtures and talk it over. Easy terms of payment, if desired.

The above offer is arranged for the months of April and May only, and positively will not be continued longer. To the first ten who avail themselves of the opportunity of wiring their homes at reduced rates, we will present an ELECTRIC FLAT IRON FREE when bill is paid in full.

CENTRAL MAINE POWER COMPANY

WATERVILLE - - MAINE

Being part of an intricate holding-company structure complicated business life for CMP. On the other hand, the Insulls came across with large supplies of cash to invest in growth. As Wyman noted, "Samuel and Martin Insull, two of the outstanding leaders in the light and power business in the world today, decided … that [CMP] common stock is good enough so that they are willing to pay $3,500,000 cash for it.… More than that — the officers of Middle West Company expect to put many more millions of dollars into [CMP] as the Company grows and needs the money."[39]

And so they did — just in time for the onset of the Depression.

← Excavation for Weston Station, Skowhegan

Turbine hall, Gulf Island

CENTRAL MAINE
POWER COMPANY

The Depression

Insull cash came to CMP from Middle West Utilities via New England Public Service Company, a mid-level holding company for Insull's regional properties, organized in the summer of 1925 with Samuel Insull as chairman and Wyman as president. Nepsco, as it was known, sold preferred stock to Middle West, and also received $12.9 million for common stock and as capital contributions.[40]

Employee sporting trophy

CMP received enough of the Nepsco capital to build the 20-megawatt Gulf Island hydroelectric plant on the Androscoggin River in Lewiston, the 72-megawatt William S. Wyman Station on the Kennebec at Bingham and Moscow, and a big storage reservoir on the Moose River.

The Gulf Island project was then the biggest in Maine. The half-mile-wide dam created a lake in the river 11 miles long and a mile and a half wide at its maximum. Each of its four generators would be as powerful as CMP's entire Deer Rips Station downstream. It was completed ahead of schedule in 1926 and under budget at about $4.5 million.

It was just a warm-up for the Bingham project on the upper Kennebec, however. The July 1928 announcement predicted the $7 million project with its 100-foot-tall dam would be ready in 1931 to provide CMP's cheapest electricity yet. Wyman said a bigger project could yield even lower kilowatt-hour costs, but the lack of a Maine market and the state law prohibiting power exports prevented it.[41] The CMP board of directors named the new project "Wyman Dam" while Wyman had stepped out of the meeting to take a phone call.[42] Pleased, he consented.

Gulf Island Station, spanning the Androscoggin →

← Overleaf: C.C. Allen's pole crew, Rockland area, 1929

Building the 72-megawatt Wyman Dam required diverting the Kennebec River, then building a concrete core wall on bedrock. Two and a half million cubic yards of earth and rock fill formed the bulk of the dam, while 260,000 cubic yards of concrete went into the power house, log sluice, spillways, and other structures. The first of its three generators went on-line in December 1930, as the dam continued backing up the waters of the Kennebec 135 feet above their normal level.[43]

Aboard the Jacona: power control room

"Past experience has shown that the Company must anticipate its growth by three or four years," Wyman had said.[44] Wyman Dam was built even further ahead of the curve, and needed some additional load to absorb part of its output and defray its costs. Wyman arranged Nepsco financing of the $10 million Maine Seaboard Paper Mill at Bucksport (later a Champion International mill) to provide that load and promote economic development.

When it was clear that the mill would be ready before the required transmission lines could be extended from Wyman Dam, he also arranged for Nepsco to buy a World War I-era cargo ship, the *Jacona*, and had it fitted out in Virginia with powerful oil-fired generators. Towed to Bucksport, the *Jacona* supplied the mill until April 1931, then was moved to Portsmouth, N.H., to augment Public Service of New Hampshire's generating capability.[45]

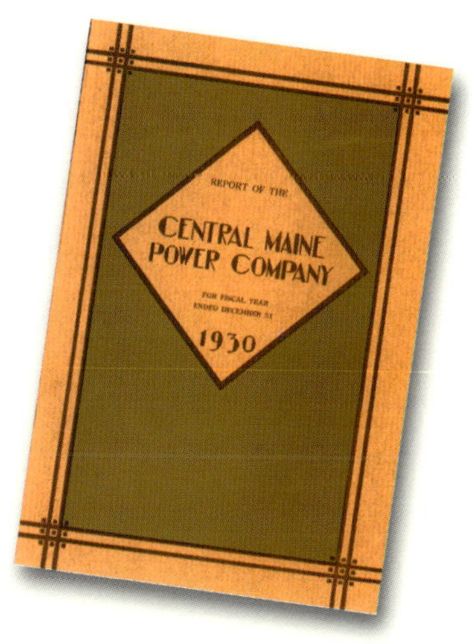

← The Jacona at Bucksport, 1930

Before the bucket truck: linemen, 1930

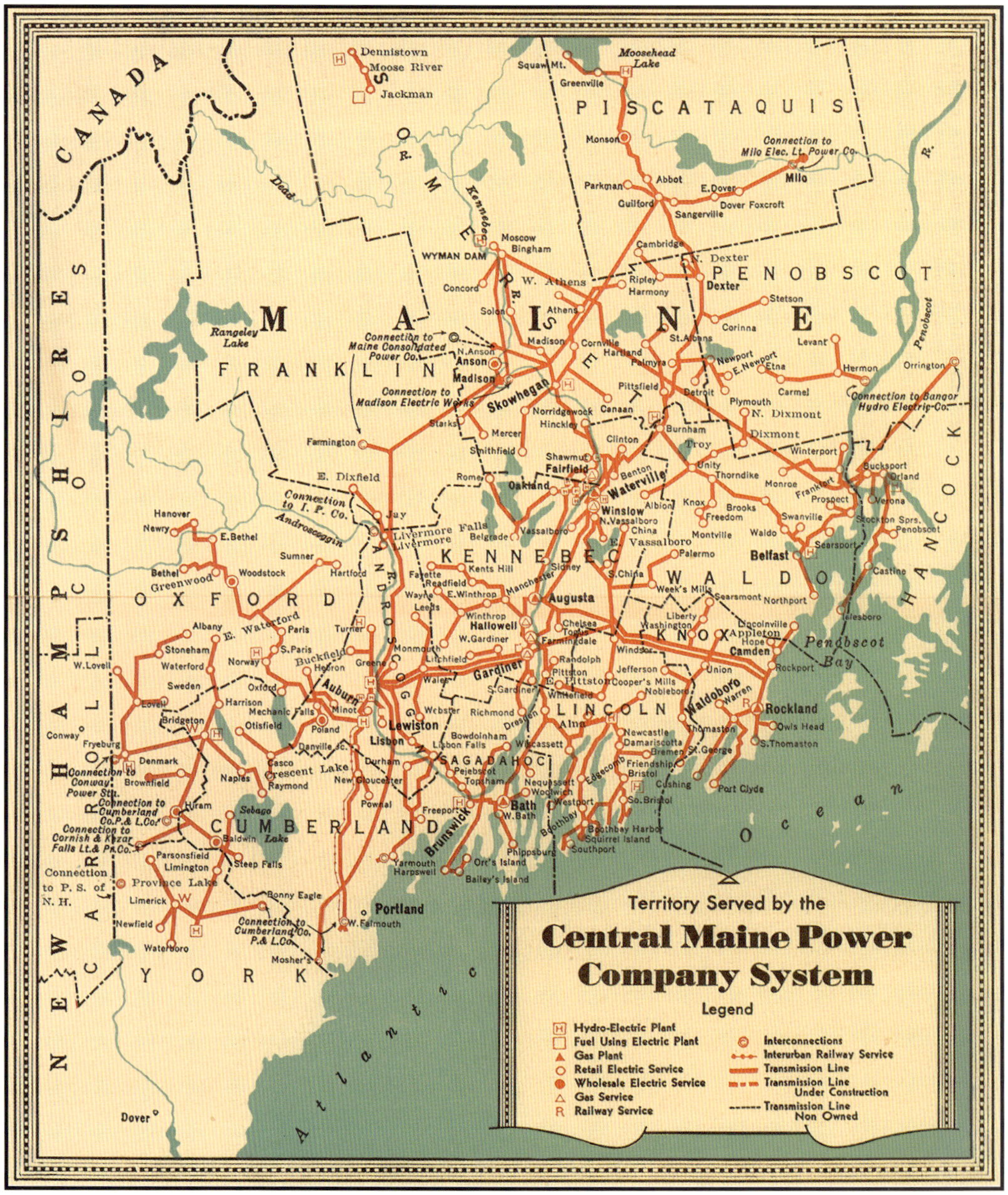

During this period of general economic expansion and CMP system expansion, localized distress required Wyman to take other extraordinary steps to preserve his vision of an integrated electric system. Cotton-textile mills had grown in places like Lewiston, Auburn, Biddeford, Saco, and Augusta in the late 1800s, and were Maine's leading industry in the 1920s. But competition from Southern mills, closer to the fiber and enjoying lower-cost labor, was driving New England mills toward bankruptcy.

Territory Served by the
Central Maine Power Company System

Legend

- Hydro-Electric Plant
- Fuel Using Electric Plant
- Gas Plant
- Retail Electric Service
- Wholesale Electric Service
- Gas Service
- Railway Service
- Interconnections
- Interurban Railway Service
- Transmission Line
- Transmission Line Under Construction
- Transmission Line Non Owned

The system, 1932: lights, gas, trolleys, buses →

← Edwards textile mill, Augusta, ca. 1930

The Truth about Rural Electrification

Issued by CENTRAL MAINE POWER CO.
W. S. WYMAN, President
W. B. SKELTON, Vice President

Lewiston's 1,000-employee Androscoggin Mills announced their intention to close in 1928; more than 2,000 other jobs at the nearby Bates and Hill mills were in jeopardy. The prospect of losing major industrial load was especially grim because the Fernald Law would prevent selling the unused energy across the state's borders. After failing to interest local investors in saving the mills, Wyman persuaded the Middle West Utilities organization to create New England Industries, Inc., in early 1929, with Nepsco holding one-third ownership. The new company carried the three Lewiston-Auburn mills, plus Augusta's Edwards mill and Saco's York mill, through the Depression years of the 1930s.

The Depression did not start at a particular hour on a particular day. Mild inflation and credit expansion stopped near the end of 1928, when the Dow-Jones Industrial Average stood at 245, and economy stopped growing by June 1929. In response, the heavily debt-financed stock market stopped advancing in September at a peak of 452. Several days' heavy stock selling in late October 1929 led to the "Black Tuesday" liquidation of October 29, with the Dow drifting to 224 by mid-November. Banks began calling loans, the Federal Reserve System began a one-third contraction of the money supply, while Congress raised taxes and enacted tariffs that stifled U.S. exports. The sharp downturn had become an entrenched deflationary crisis that depressed prices and wages. U.S. unemployment jumped from 3 percent in 1929 to nearly 27 percent in 1934. Economic output didn't exceed 1929 levels more than temporarily until late 1941, when rearmament programs spurred by the threats of Nazi Germany and Imperial Japan finally restored the flow of cash and credit.[46]

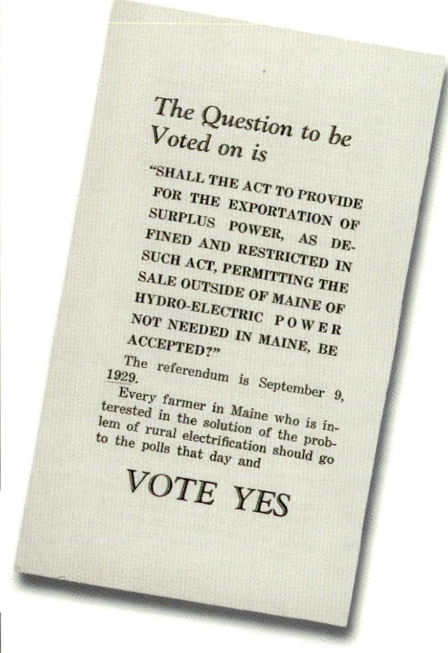
The Question to be Voted on is

"SHALL THE ACT TO PROVIDE FOR THE EXPORTATION OF SURPLUS POWER, AS DEFINED AND RESTRICTED IN SUCH ACT, PERMITTING THE SALE OUTSIDE OF MAINE OF HYDRO-ELECTRIC POWER NOT NEEDED IN MAINE, BE ACCEPTED?"

The referendum is September 9, 1929.

Every farmer in Maine who is interested in the solution of the problem of rural electrification should go to the polls that day and

VOTE YES

Innovations and adaptations

CMP's growth in 1920s and '30s was more than a matter of absorbing smaller electric companies and extending lines. It also included new ways of doing business and new services.

One new service was improved communication with customers. A CMP Speakers Bureau was organized in May 1927, initially with 18 members including Wyman himself, who offered to speak to groups on "Maine's Water Power." Ralph Bragg offered "The Romance of the Gas Industry," outlining CMP's small manufactured-gas operations. Other talks included an explanation of electric meters, a demonstration of artificial resuscitation, and young William Wyman's description of the electric-distribution business.[r]

In July 1927, CMP's Rural Service Department joined the University of Maine's College of Agriculture in the first of a series of demonstration farm remodelings. The Charles C. Clement and Son poultry farm in Winterport enjoyed a new, 12,000-chick electric incubator — coal and oil fueled its two existing units — as well as electric heaters for the fowls' drinking water in winter.

Building on the 1929 appliance-demonstrating success of the Home Service Work Department with its popular demonstration kitchens, a Home Lighting Department started up in 1934 with "four girls and a supervisor." Eulalie Collins and her staff were trained and equipped with Sight-Meters and General Electric lighting kits to advise homemakers on proper lighting levels, lamps, and shades. "A few cents a day on your lighting bill," the *Exciter* editorialized, "may be the difference between good eyesight, and bad."

Technical innovations were adopted as well. Meter Engineer Merton Taylor used spare parts to construct his own lineman's-glove testing device in 1927. Taylor's apparatus used a chain energized at 11,000 volts inside a water-filled rubber glove, which was suspended in a grounded test tank. Instruments measured any current leakage through minute holes or tears.

Regular equipment testing using newer technology and tightly regulated safety standards continues as standard practice today.

The year 1927 also brought a productivity enhancement to the arduous work of digging holes and setting electric poles. A new digging machine operated by two workers could excavate an 24-inch-wide, eight-foot-deep hole and set a 40-foot pole in less than 10 minutes, if there was no ledge. Meanwhile, the increasing numbers and complexity of street lights and traffic lights made climbing poles, setting up ladders, or lowering suspended units for maintenance increasingly tedious and dangerous. “A very useful and worthwhile piece of equipment” was tested in Augusta in 1936: a half-ton Chevrolet truck with a 24-foot ladder that could be swiveled in a complete circle and raised to the level of the street light, even if cars were parked in the way. It was a precursor to the hydraulic-arm bucket trucks that tend to such work today.

Some innovations were cosmetic. Lewiston’s five meter readers of 1937, responsible for nearly 19,000 meters, “some of them being found in cellars, coal bins, attic rooms, and many other hidden places,” were testing new uniforms. “Similar in color to the State Police,” the uniforms included a short military-style jacket, tie, and for three of the men, knee-high boots and cavalry-style trousers with flared thighs. Although the *Exciter* reported many compliments and the advantage that “Customers know at a glance that it is the meter reader at the door and not some boy selling magazines,” this innovation did not endure.[5]

Depression - era measures included promotional rates like 1936’s 1-cent per kilowatt-hour electric water-heating rate for homes using more than 200 kilowatt-hours a month (not a big audience — the average home used 600 a year). New appliance-sales drives also helped relieve the revenue sting of lower rates and slack industrial demand: 1937’s total of 19,548 appliances included eight garbage disposals and a soil heater.

Innovation never stops, of course. Two-way CMP radio stations were set up in Augusta and Portland in 1949, allowing supervisors and line crews to relay trouble calls and information from their vehicles. Today, work orders can be transmitted to computers in line trucks, and crews can fill in details and return forms electronically. Substations that once required manual operation now automatically report their loads and can be automatically controlled from remote locations. Meter readers’ pads and pencils have been replaced by hand-held computers that disgorge their readings directly into another computer. So it goes, with more surprises to come.

No pad, no pencil: meter reader’s computer

A tangle of trolley wires, ca. 1930

The Depression had no large, immediate impact on CMP. The 1928 crisis in the Maine textile industry and the 1929 referendum preserving the state's ban on hydro-power exports were bigger issues of the moment. Electricity sales rose 12 percent from 1929 to 1930, for example, and revenues rose 11 percent despite another rate cut of about 8 percent overall. Annual residential usage rose from 386 kilowatt-hours in 1929 to 438 kwh in 1930.[47]

Both residential customer count and kilowatt-hour usage continued to rise through the '30s, ending at 75,366 residential customers with an average usage of 746 kwh in 1939. CMP could also boast of substantial progress in bringing power to farms. By mid-1930, 8,400 or almost 17 percent of Maine's 53,000 farms had electricity, compared to a national average of 6 percent.[48]

In an October 1, 1930, letter to CMP shareholders, Wyman wrote, "Your Company enters the last quarter of 1930 in very good shape." Construction at Bingham was nearly complete and its financing was nearly settled. "A great many of the mills and factories in Maine are running full time and employing the usual number of men," he added. "Although a very decided business depression exists nationally, I think we are more fortunate than many of the other states in this respect."

There were problems, nonetheless, and they would grow.

Dapper at Wyman Hydro dedication, 1931, a year before the Insull empire collapsed: Director Carroll Perkins, President Walter Wyman, Chairman Martin Insull, V.P. William Skelton

The debt-financed Insull holding-company structure began to collapse as its revenues fell and bankers called in loans. Samuel Insull fled the country under indictment. Martin Insull resigned as chairman of the CMP board in 1932, while the company's net income fell by 30 percent in 1932 and by another 30 percent in 1933.

Middle West's financial vulnerability had not gone unnoticed. Writing in 1927, Bowdoin College economist Orren Hormell noted that Middle West had issued debt equivalent to more than 99 percent of its assets and was deriving more than 40 percent of its income from selling securities. Hormell warned, "A decline in the general price level, a severe financial depression, or even unfavorable or efficient regulation by state commissions might wipe out much of the value back of the securities of the holding companies."[49] And so it had.

Wyman — who had wisely never lent money "upstream" in the Insull structure, as some other operating utilities had — used his resources and personal influence to mount another rescue operation. Organizing friendly investors as the Northern New England Company, he bought back Nepsco stock, with its control of CMP, from Insull's creditors. Other drastic actions followed. The Lewiston-Portland Interurban trolley operation was closed down with a million-dollar write-off in 1933. CMP common-stock dividends were discontinued in 1933, and preferred dividends were halved in 1934.

Wyman had his own financial problems in this period. He and newspaper publisher Guy Gannett were major backers of the 14-bank system centered on the Fidelity Trust Company of Portland. Fidelity was one of thousands of banks that failed around the country in 1933. Unlike many others, it reopened after Franklin Roosevelt's "bank holiday" of inspection and restructuring, and eventually restored 94 percent of its investors' capital.[50]

Yet the company persevered. Besides saving the five textile mills, it helped sustain Keyes Fibre Company in Waterville and the Bath Iron Works in difficult times. It survived increased taxes — including the new 1937 obligation to contribute to Social Security on behalf of employees (who were taxed 1 percent of pay for their share). In 1937, CMP shut down Wyman's one-time employer, the Waterville, Fairfield and Oakland Railway, and scrapped its equipment at a $446,000 loss.

Franklin D. Roosevelt's electric pathway to your parlor

Management took pay cuts and other economy measures were put in place. The size, frequency, and production values of the newsletter were reduced, and it carried exhortations against wasting stationery and paper clips. Employee outings were postponed. Sales campaigns for appliances and wiring were intensified. Thanks to such efforts, CMP Vice President George Williams could say in 1938, "It has been possible to keep our permanent employees working steadily at the present wage scale, which to our mind is the last thing to be affected."[51]

Mason Station at full tilt for the war effort →

Part of Mason Station crew, 1941

Staff Sergeant Edward Conley, Jr.: from CMP's Augusta store to an air base in India.

There was still room for hustle, however. In the pre-war summer of 1939, Junior Appliance Salesman Edwin Jones of the Rockland office was "making the old timers sit up and take notice" as he bustled about in a Dodge pickup truck specially outfitted to display lamps and appliances. Young Jones moved $72.79 of merchandise in his first week on the road, including sales of 77 lamps, three electric flat irons, and five electric bug killers.[52]

On a larger scale, the 1930s' need for operating economy did not stop construction. The million-dollar Williams hydro station in Solon came on-line in 1939, with its first unit rated at 7 megawatts. And in 1940, work was begun on a 20-megawatt steam plant at Wiscasset, to be called Mason Station. The new steam project reflected both Wyman's belief that it was imprudent to be wholly at the mercy of hydro conditions, and his belief that war might erupt in Europe and require more power for Maine industry.[53]

An accelerating federal defense build-up was already under way in 1940, including aid to the beleaguered United Kingdom, and it grew more intense during 1941, the year that closed with the December 7 Japanese attack on Pearl Harbor, Hawaii, and brought the United States into the Second World

War. Mason Station came on-line just three weeks later, consuming 250 tons of soft coal daily to add to the supply of power for industry.

The Depression was over when Walter Wyman wrote his last annual-report letter to CMP shareholders. Yet, "Taking everything into account," he said, "the year 1941 presented the most difficult operating problems which this Company has ever faced." A drought had hurt hydro-unit performance, taxes had risen, and the government's huge defense purchases were creating shortages of vital materials.

William Skelton,
President 1942-1947

Wyman suffered one heart attack in June 1941 and another in January 1942. He grew weaker as the year advanced, but conducted business at home in his study or from his sickbed. He died on November 15, 1942. Maine newspapers lavished editorial praise on Wyman. "Mr. Wyman was a savior of industry as well as a builder of it," said the Portland *Press Herald*. Wyman's rescue of Keyes Fibre and Bath Iron Works, the Bath *Times* said, "showed he loved his state so strongly that he contributed much to its prosperity." The Lewiston *Evening Journal* judged that Wyman "contributed much to the industrial progress of many Maine communities, and to his efforts many Maine citizens owe their opportunities for employment." The Bangor *Commercial* called him "an executive to whose genius Maine owes much of its industrial progress."[54] There were more tributes in the same vein — high praise for anyone, including a small-town boy whose father worked in a tool factory.

By the time of Walter Wyman's death, the U.S. Navy had inflicted a crushing defeat on the Japanese fleet at Midway, the British had checked the German-Italian forces threatening the Suez Canal, and the Red Army was preparing to encircle more than 250,000 Axis soldiers in a frozen, ruined city called Stalingrad. Allied victory in the world war, though not assured, now seemed likely. CMP, with long-time vice president William B. Skelton succeeding Wyman, supported the war effort and saw in the nation's growing economic revival the seeds of resurgence.

Technical Sergeant Carleton "Bill" Doak, on loan to Uncle Sam from CMP's Plant Department

The Resurgence

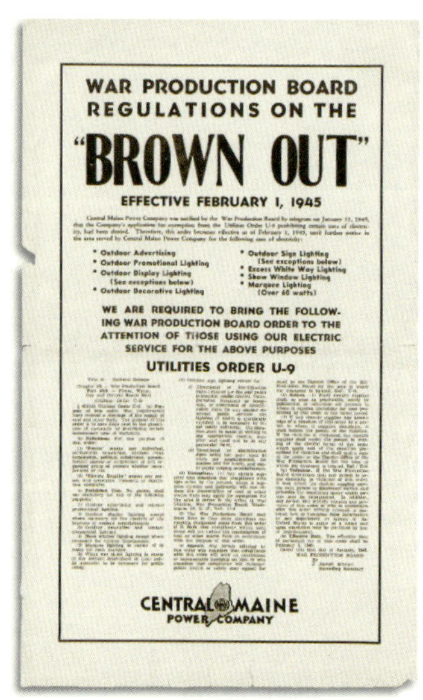

WAR PRODUCTION BOARD REGULATIONS ON THE

"BROWN OUT"

EFFECTIVE FEBRUARY 1, 1945

Central Maine Power Company was notified by the War Production Board by telegram on January 11, 1945, that the Company's application for exemption from the Utilities Order U-9 prohibiting certain uses of electricity, had been denied. Therefore, this order becomes effective as of February 1, 1945, until further notice in the area served by Central Maine Power Company for the following uses of electricity:

- Outdoor Advertising
- Outdoor Promotional Lighting
- Outdoor Display Lighting (See exceptions below)
- Outdoor Decorative Lighting
- Outdoor Sign Lighting (See exceptions below)
- Excess White Way Lighting
- Show Window Lighting
- Marquee Lighting (Over 60 watts)

WE ARE REQUIRED TO BRING THE FOLLOWING WAR PRODUCTION BOARD ORDER TO THE ATTENTION OF THOSE USING OUR ELECTRIC SERVICE FOR THE ABOVE PURPOSES

UTILITIES ORDER U-9

[illegible]

CENTRAL MAINE POWER COMPANY

Defense workers' friend: a CMP bus

← Overleaf: Line workers up-country, 1940s

Less than three weeks after the death of Walter Wyman, CMP took a huge step in growth. The Cumberland County Power and Light Company was merged into CMP effective December 3, 1942. Thirty-seven cities and towns were added to the electric service area; the additions included gas customers in Biddeford and Saco, and riders for CCP&L's fleet of 68 buses plying the streets of Portland, South Portland, and Westbrook.

The companies had become affiliates through the Insull entry into Maine in 1925, and had shared power and facilities. But the formal merger made CMP the largest electric utility in northern New England, and positioned it for eventual large-scale connection to the rest of New England.

The demands of the war affected nearly every aspect of life, not sparing CMP. Gasoline and tires were rationed, so employees were urged to walk or bike to work. Some rural customers were sent post cards to mail back with meter readings to save driving. All 957 employees were fingerprinted under federal rules for vital industries. In late 1942, only eighteen refrigerators were allotted for CMP's appliance stores, which had orders for 300. As in the first World War, women joined the ranks of meter readers. Like other employers, CMP exhorted employees to expand food production with backyard Victory Gardens and to buy War Bonds.

Bucksport store promotes War Bonds

Facilities were secured and prepared for the worst. "In the event that Adolph [Hitler] decides Lewiston is a likely bombing target," the *Exciter* reported, the appliance store would serve as air- raid shelter and medical station.[55]

The CMP newsletter editorialized, "We're an army — almost 1,000 strong. The army of the home front. Our fighting front is 6,177 miles of power lines in the Central Maine territory. Generators, substations, cut-outs, switches, safety belts, hi-lines, dams, steam plants, trucks, typewriters, pencils, and meters are our weapons. We fight wind, rain, lightning, snow, sleet, kites, floods—enemies that bullets and bombs can't kill. It's our job to make sure that dependable power turns out the ships, the shoes, the cloth for uniforms, the machines, the parts for bombs and bullets that our soldiers and sailors need to win this war."[56]

Uncle Sam Asks Farmers to

Step Up Milk Production

WE HAVE A LIMITED STOCK of MILK COOLERS—
Visit our nearest store and obtain information about buying and installing an electric Milk Cooler. No obligation.

When you produce extra milk for our population and armed forces, you are rendering a patriotic service of great importance. But, before you can step up production you must be equipped to handle the larger quantity with minimum work and worry. An electric milk cooler is one of your best allies in this respect. Come in for further details; and also obtain information about poultry equipment and water systems.

CENTRAL MAINE POWER COMPANY

Farmers are becoming acquainted with Reddy Kilowatt through the Company's ads on the back cover of "Electricity on the Farm."

More than 300 CMP employees served in the armed forces during the war. Most returned to the company. But Lawrence Gammon, Carman Ladner, Burnell Mank, Robert Morang, Orville Nisbet, Burleigh Roderick, Richard Warren, and Thomas Whitney died on Italian hills, Pacific islands, and other foreign ground. After the Japanese surrender in September 1945 ended World War II, the *Exciter* paid tribute to their sacrifice and optimistically gave thanks for "mounting evidence which seems to point the way to universal peace forever hereafter."

Transformers arriving at Louden substation, 1951 →

Promoting new electronic range

CMP had built new power plants and substations to handle increased load from defense industries, including Bath Iron Works and the New England Shipbuilding yards in South Portland. But wartime rationing had made expansion of CMP's normal business difficult: new appliances and copper wire were scarce. Home electrification was one of the few sales opportunities available. Starting in 1942, "two full-time girls" and four other Home Service Advisers began promoting new developments in lighting equipment and methods.

CMP's York Office

Postwar pent-up demand for homes and consumer goods, plus returning servicemen and -women starting new families, partially offset the drop in electric load from defense industry. During the week of April 21, 1947, the Portland Exposition Building hosted the first postwar Modern Homes Show. More than 40,000 people attended, and CMP Home Service Adviser Jean Parsons "was literally swamped by interested spectators who crowded her [display] kitchen every time she demonstrated the new GE range or dishwasher.[57]

CMP took advantage of the renewed availability of copper wire to push line extensions in rural areas. About 1,300 miles of extensions were planned in 1946-47, tripling the pace of the war years. The aim was to bring electric service to 90 percent of the farms in CMP's service area, up from 75 percent before the war — but even that was double the national average.[58]

The Maloy and Foss pump power at South Portland, 1947

Having sold its Cumberland County bus line in 1944, CMP liquidated its industrial investments in 1946, earning $6.5 million on Wyman's original load-rescuing investment. CMP common stock began public trading on the New York Stock Exchange in 1946, ticker symbol "CTP" (the symbol survives, but now designates the common stock of CMP Group).

In a reprise of the *Jacona* innovation, CMP dealt with drought-induced hydro shortages in 1947 by arranging "Operation Kilowatt." The Navy destroyer escorts *Maloy* and *Foss* tied up at the South Portland shipyard pier in November 1947 and were wired into the shipyard substation. Burning 30,000 gallons of oil a day, each ship ran engines at the equivalent of 21 knots to supply 4,500 kilowatts of power for the CMP grid until March 1948.[59] Meanwhile, CMP steam plants at Portland, Bucksport, Lewiston, Wiscasset, and Biddeford also ran flat-out to meet demand.

Troubleshooter in truck, ca. 1950

Operation Kilowatt and CMP's collection of steam plants underscored the wisdom of Wyman's desire to diversify generation sources. But hydroelectric power was still the core of the CMP system — 90 percent of capacity as late as 1945.[60] And it continued to expand. A major construction project

90 miles north of Augusta at the confluence of the Kennebec and Dead Rivers — another site Wyman had picked early on for future development — created the Indian Pond storage reservoir behind a 175-foot-high dam. The 75-megawatt power station, named for Chief Engineer Ford Harris, was dedicated in 1953. The Indian Pond storage also allowed installing a second generator at the 1939-vintage Williams hydro station in Solon; Wyman had it built with a second bay available for future use.

Canco Road service center, Portland

Big power plants were still the way to satisfy rising electric demand. And the federal government's policy of promoting peaceful uses of atomic energy was making new power options available. Taking a 9.5 percent stake in the first New England nuclear project, CMP joined 11 other utilities in 1954 to form Yankee Atomic Electric Company, which would build a small reactor in Rowe, Massachusetts. Recognizing the trend toward more regional transactions in power, the Maine Legislature finally repealed the Fernald Law in 1955. That same year, CMP began construction of the oil-fired W. F. Wyman station on Cousins Island in Yarmouth.

Construction at Cousins Island →

But the accustomed sequence of utility economics — new plant, lower unit costs, lower rates for customers — was no longer a sure thing. In May 1948, the costs of dealing with postwar inflation and poor hydro conditions had led CMP to seek an 8 percent rate increase, the first such request in more than 30 years. The PUC found it justified. Price increases would no longer be rarities.

William Wyman,
President 1947-1962

Other aspects of the business were changing as well. William Skelton retired from CMP's presidency in 1947 to become chairman of the board of directors. He was succeeded as president by William F. Wyman. The Harvard-educated son of the co-founder had spent more than 20 years working his way up through the ranks.

In 1949, the 50th anniversary of the enterprise, CMP exited the small and economically marginal coal-gas business. In 1958, more than four decades of appliance merchandising stopped; the CMP stores were losing money, and they invited accusations of unfair competition during rate proceedings. CMP decided instead to concentrate on promoting the use of electricity.

← Electric-laundry display at Lewiston store, 1949

Meter reader Alice Sweetland

Women at CMP

Most of the jobs in CMP's early years were the exclusive domain of men: linemen, power-plant operators, engineers, executives. Even the president's stenographer was a man.

As time passed, more women worked at the company, though typically as secretaries and clerks. For years, the company sponsored a "CMP Girls Club" and women employees were routinely characterized as "girls" or "gals" in newsletter articles.

One early exception to the stereotypes was Alice Sweetland, who became CMP's first woman meter reader in 1918.

"There weren't any men around," she told an interviewer long afterwards. "They were all off fighting World War I."[1] Then a 20-year-old fresh out of business college, Alice took the opportunity to do something different for $10 a week.

She read about 2,100 meters a month, riding a trolley to West Gardiner or Farmingdale, then walking back with her notebook and pencil to read meters on the way. "The hardest part of the job was that the meters were inside the house in those days," she said.

CMP athletic team, 1919

Office-machinery operator, ca. 1940

At some locations, "I'd have to climb up four flights of stairs to read the electric meter, then walk down to the cellar where the gas meter was. There were days when it took two people to pull off my boots."

For her Pittston meters, Alice would take the CMP mare "Old Molly" and a cart. She was told to read all the meters on the outbound leg of the Pittston trip: once Old Molly turned around, she could not be made to stop until she was back in the comfort of her stable.

Alice read meters for a year, then transferred to work in the treasury and accounting departments until her retirement in 1953. She considered her duties "the worst, ruggedest job a woman ever had," but said she did as well as any man — "no question in my mind."

Such questions seldom rise today. CMP has 38 women in management positions, including President Sara Burns, Corporate Secretary Anne Paré, Human Resources Director Kathleen Case, Environment and Licensing Director Mary R. Smith, and Operations Managers Constance Hayward in Augusta and Carol Purinton in Brunswick. Nearly 200 women hold jobs in finance and administration, as well as in positions as engineers, environmental specialists, computer technicians and meter readers. Others have served as vice presidents for marketing and communications.

Women account for 36 percent of CMP's current workforce of 1,590 people. That's progress in a traditionally male-dominated industry, but still a ways from resembling the larger society. The company uses active monitoring and recruitment to bolster the ranks of women and to ensure that no qualified candidate misses out on a CMP job opportunity because of her gender.

In the field, 1990s

Customer-service representative

William Dunham,
President 1962-1972

Ruth Warren, (right) televising the appeal of electric cooking, ca. 1955 →

Electricity-sales campaigns weren't new, but the late-'50s and early-'60s efforts included coordination with nationwide advertising campaigns by electric-utility and home-building trade groups. Consumers across the country were encouraged to "Live Better Electrically" and to dwell in "Medallion Homes." CMP's minimum standards for applying a bronze medallion to a home included having 100-amp service, a range and at least three other major electric appliances, and wall-switched ceiling lights at room entrances. Total-electric homes, including electric heat, qualified for a gold medallion. In the first four months of 1959, 31 bronze and two gold medallions were awarded to CMP customers. A special CMP rate enhanced the appeal of the electric-heat option. A CMP Area Development Department was launched in 1963 to promote expansion of agriculture, industry, natural-resource development and recreation in Maine.

More price promotions followed. In 1964, CMP added incentives for upgrading electric-service amperage and for building or converting homes with electric heat. Rates also reflected the declining unit costs of increased output. By 1966, the "declining block" charges for residential service fell to 1.5 cents per kilowatt-hour for customers with above-average usage, and promotional incentives were paid for purchases of 4,900 electric dryers and 2,500 electric water heaters in that year.

The '60s were a transition period for CMP. President William F. Wyman died in 1962 at age 59, and was succeeded by Vice President William H. Dunham. The new CEO was a Bates College and Cornell Law School graduate who had joined the organization in 1939 as a lawyer on the New England Public Service Company staff. He led CMP through critical decisions in the nuclear era, and saw the CMP-led Maine Yankee project go into operation near the end of his tenure.

Checking out a bucket truck

A new era in corporate governance at CMP began January 20, 1966, when Bates College president and nationally known economist Charles F. Phillips was elected chairman of the board of directors. Dr. Phillips, who joined the board in 1953 and retired in 1980, was its first "outside" chairman. The advantages of CMP's outside chairman and outside-director majority during problems with CEOs in 1983 and 1991 were favorably noted in a *Wall Street Journal* article.[61]

Base rates were reduced for five straight years through 1967, and an adjustment to the "fuel clause" pass-through allowed another small reduction in 1968. The average CMP customer was using seven times as much electricity as in 1930, but at a 55 percent lower price.[62] The average residential customer used 4,200 kilowatt-hours a year at an average unit price of 1.88 cents — cheap by any standard.

A faster, safer way to the top

← Putting meters through their paces (most defectives run slow, if at all)

Besides enjoying another spell of fair weather in rates, CMP customers were spared the immense disruption that spread across most of the Northeast in just four seconds at 5:16 PM on November 9, 1965. A transmission line near Niagara Falls, New York, tripped out, overloading five others in the area and isolating 1,800 megawatts of generation at Niagara. Deprived of load, the units became unstable and shut down, breaking power-system integration for the entire Northeast and Ontario within four seconds. Outages spread and remaining "islands" of power blacked out within five minutes. From Ontario to parts of Pennsylvania and New Jersey, some 30 million people were in the dark for up to 13 hours.[63] CMP's weak connections with the regional grid at that time broke down almost instantly, but a rapid response by dispatchers kept load aligned with generation and the lights on. Nonetheless, the event fueled many people's apprehensions about the vulnerability of large, technologically complex systems. CMP responded by joining other New England utilities in the 1966 decision to organize the New England Power Pool and the New England Power Exchange. The organizations would be responsible for joint planning of power supply and transmission, and for conducting economics-based dispatch of regional generation.

Mainframe computing, ca. 1965

Other forces would change the economics of power production and the expectations of electric customers. Rachel Carson, a federal marine biologist, published *Silent Spring* in 1962. The book warned of the hazards of widespread pesticide use and helped build public support for measures like the National Environmental Policy Act of 1969, which required environmental-impact statements as part of the power-plant permitting process, and for the Clean Air Act of 1970. The political landscape would also change as the U.S. combat role in Vietnam grew in the late 1960s. Seeds of other troubles were sown in the Middle East, where's Israel's six-day defeat of an Arab coalition in June 1967 left the defeated states looking for a rematch with their oil reserves used as a strategic weapon against the West.

Developments in the domestic utility business would also shape future events. The Massachusetts Yankee nuclear plant successfully went into commercial operation on July 1, 1961. CMP followed up with financial commitments for other nuclear plants: Connecticut Yankee, Vermont Yankee, Maine Yankee. The attractions of nuclear power for CMP included the limited remaining potential for Maine hydro development, federal support of civilian nuclear energy, and an end to the big efficiency gains traditionally achieved as bigger oil-fired plants were built.[64]

Elwin Thurlow
President 1972-1983

As CMP entered the 1970s, the momentum was still with growth. The New England Power Pool began formal operations in June 1970, with CMP participation. In 1971, the last phase of a 345,000-volt transmission tie between New Brunswick and CMP's grid allowed increased electricity imports from Canada. President William Dunham told CMP shareholders at the 1971 annual meeting that CMP sales would rise and that by the year 2000, "Improved nuclear energy in the form of breeder and fusion reactors should be able to supply all our energy needs for centuries."[65]

Dunham became chairman of the company of CMP, while Elwin W. Thurlow, a former meter reader who had won a Distinguished Flying Cross in World War II service and risen through the engineering ranks after returning to CMP, succeeded him as president.

The last year of CMP's postwar resurgence may have been 1972. The Vermont Yankee and Maine Yankee nuclear plants began commercial operation. Planning was underway for a 600-megawatt addition to the oil-fired W.F. Wyman Station in Yarmouth. Design work also started on Boston Edison's Pilgrim Unit 2 nuclear plant, in which CMP held a 2.85 percent interest.

Finally, in 1972, CMP announced that it would invest in a two-reactor project led by the Public Service Company of New Hampshire. The big new nuclear plants, over 1,100 megawatts each, would be built in a coastal town called Seabrook.

The Gauntlet

A gauntlet of problems faced Americans in 1973, including political upheaval and fears about energy supply. The now-unpopular Indochina war continued, and the Nixon presidency was struggling to contain investigations of illegal break-ins and cover-ups. A new Arab-Israeli war erupted in the Middle East, and an embargo by Arab oil-producing states drove petroleum prices skyward.

A 1973 referendum campaign urged Maine voters to approve creation of a Power Authority of Maine with the ability to buy or purchase generation and transmission facilities. CMP's Bill Dunham told a legislative committee that the PAM proposal was "the most extreme, radical, and socialistic plan for attempted state entry into power supply and takeover of private business that exists anywhere in the nation."[66] The authority would be largely uncontrolled, he said, and its alleged cost advantage would lie mainly in its claimed exemption from the taxes paid by investor-owned utilities, that would have to be made up somewhere else. Voters defeated the proposal, and it did not resurface.

But the October 1973 Middle East war had lasting impacts. When Arab oil states stopped exports to countries supporting Israel, the oil supply reaching world markets plunged by 4 million barrels a day. Average crude-oil prices jumped from $3 a barrel in 1972 to $12 by the end of 1974, and to $14 by the end of 1978.[67] Western economies tipped into recession. Federal price controls (not lifted until 1981) were imposed on domestic oil, with the unintended effects of creating shortages, gas lines, reduced incentives to explore, and an enduring perception of an "energy crisis." When revolution overthrew the Shah of Iran in 1979 and created another severe disruption in oil supply, President Jimmy Carter took to the airwaves wearing a cardigan sweater to declare the energy situation "the moral equivalent of war" and encouraging Americans to conserve.

The energy-market disruptions of the '70s had three implications for CMP: they boosted the appeal of nuclear power, increased the pressure to sponsor energy-conservation programs, and fueled the political drive toward developing new energy sources that did not rely on oil.

← Oil crises: gas lines, inflation, new energy policies, and more (Corbis/Bettmann)

In the midst of the oil-induced recession of 1974-75, CMP president Thurlow called nuclear plants "pathways to the future," predicting that in 10 years, nuclear power would meet 72 percent of CMP's energy needs, and that peak demand would reach 1,967 megawatts. For a variety of reasons, especially the effects of rising prices, those supply-planners' projections never played out: peak demand reached only 1,288 megawatts in 1984, and nuclear power was only 28 percent of the energy mix.

But the public supported the idea. At a public forum in Searsport on January 30, 1975, CMP explained the benefits of building a new nuclear plant on Sears Island, to be 70 percent owned by Maine utilities (Maine Yankee was 50 percent Maine-owned). Residents endorsed the proposal at their March 10 town meeting by a vote of 532 to 182.[68] The sentiment wasn't just driven by local-development interests. A 1975 poll by Louis Harris Associates found 63 percent of the American public supported building more nuclear plants, while only 19 percent opposed them. Fully 78 percent of the public thought the country faced "serious energy shortages," and 38 percent thought the shortages would be "very serious." Perhaps ominously, 56 percent of environmentalists, 72 percent of regulators, and 78 percent of political leaders leaned to the "very serious" view of the future.[69]

Maine Yankee: more than $1 billion cheaper than burning oil

Inspecting General Office bomb damage, 1976

Maine Yankee's reactor vessel reports for duty

CMP cooperated with new policies stressing energy efficiency and reduced reliance on imported oil. The Kilowatt Savings Time program appeared in 1976; on days of high load, it asked customers to shift usage to evening hours to reduce the use of oil-fired power plants designed for peaking rather than base-load operation. CMP tested ceramic-block heaters that used off-peak electricity, and reminded customers of tax credits for weatherization and renewable-resource energy installations. CMP's spending on these and other "Demand-Side Management" or DSM programs has been as high as $17 million a year; approved utility costs for DSM were factored into rates.

In the midst of social and economic upheaval, terrorism struck CMP. The Edison Drive headquarters was evacuated shortly after 3 PM on May 11, 1976, because two phone calls warned of bombs in the building. One device exploded in the first-floor machine room, another in a third-floor library area. No one was injured, but the blasts caused extensive damage and anxiety. The perpetrators, members of a small left-wing, anti-establishment group, were arrested several years later for attacks in other states, tried, and jailed.

To mark the national-bicentennial year of 1976, CMP's annual report to shareholders featured photos of a musket-toting Minuteman in the Maine Yankee control room and other venues. Nuclear energy reached a peak at 47 percent of CMP's energy mix that year. But difficulties were growing. Technical studies at Sears Island had found the site geologically unsuited for the 1,150-megawatt nuclear station originally planned, so CMP engineers proposed a 500-to-600-megawatt coal plant instead. Site preparation finally started in July 1976 after four years of protests and delays.

As the year ended, President Thurlow called talk of zero growth in energy usage "unrealistic"; CMP estimated sales growth at 6.5 percent annually over the coming 10 years (it turned to be slightly over 4 percent compounded). It was "foolhardy" to rely on conservation and exotic technologies to meet increased demand, Thurlow said, but governmental restrictions had stalled the Sears Island project, restricted the use of coal, and limited the development of Maine's remaining hydro resources.[70] In January 1977, construction at Seabrook stopped for seven months of legal battles when the U.S. Environmental Protection Agency revoked its approval of the cooling-system design. The delay prompted CMP's outside auditors to add a cautionary clause in the annual report.

Managing load by public appeal: Kilowatt Savings Time

Meanwhile, inflation-driven interest rates and regulatory policy combined with delays at the Seabrook project to undermine CMP's finances. The company reported $1.87 earnings per share in 1977, but only $1 of it was cash. Nearly half the reported earnings were a non-cash "Allowance for Funds Used during Construction," an accounting convention intended to reflect the asset-building value of construction projects without charging customers for costs until the plants came into use. Non-cash earnings can't pay invoices or dividends, of course, so delays and cost increases in projects inevitably led to greater borrowing needs and weaker credit ratings.

Destruction but no injuries, 1976 bombing

Political opposition and regulatory proceedings continued to bedevil Seabrook and its investors. By May 1978, the anti-nuclear Clamshell Alliance had 11 chapters in Maine. The New Hampshire mother organization of Clamshell was organizing a flotilla of canoes, kayaks, rafts, and other craft to protest and prevent the scheduled barge delivery of the Seabrook reactor vessel. Alliance members picketed a July public hearing of the Maine PUC on a CMP rate request. Inside, nearly half of the 37 public witnesses expressed anti-nuclear concerns, and a third said they used no electricity in their homes.[71] Public sentiment grew increasingly skeptical of nuclear plants after a March 1979 testing mistake caused a partial fuel melt at the Three Mile Island nuclear plant near Harrisburg, Pennsylvania. Intense media coverage, aided by poor communications from plant owners and public officials, helped raise fears of a "China syndrome" meltdown through the containment vessel or a hydrogen-gas explosion. The reactor did not explode or melt down, and no one was injured, but "TMI" became a rallying cry for nuclear critics.[72]

The TMI boost to nuclear-power concerns led in September 1980 to the first of three referendum votes on closing the Maine Yankee nuclear plant at Wiscasset. Federal law prevailed in most areas affecting nuclear power, but a public no-confidence vote would be a serious matter. The 1980 vote was 59 to 41 percent for keeping the plant open. Another referendum in November 1982 would draw 56

percent support, and a final referendum in 1987 found 59 percent of voters supporting Maine Yankee. Still, the non-stop struggle for public support was a major draw on CMP's time and resources, and controversy had already persuaded the company in 1978 not to plan or join any additional nuclear projects.[73]

As problems were mounting on the nuclear side of the industry, the federal government weighed into the policy arena with the National Energy Act of 1978. The act comprised statutes dealing with conservation, taxes, industrial fuels, and other matters, but the part that would most affect CMP and its customers was the Public Utility Regulatory Policies Act (16 U.S. Code, Chap. 46), known as PURPA.

Section 210 of PURPA required electric utilities to interconnect with and buy energy that might be offered by "qualifying facilities," meaning renewable-resource power plants, municipal-waste incinerators, and some industrial cogeneration plants that produced both electricity and steam for industrial or other uses. The law also exempted most non-utility generators from federal rate and accounting regulation, as well as from federal holding-company and state utility-commission regulations, and required that utilities pay for the energy at no more than the "avoided cost" of supplying the energy through their own resources. Otherwise, implementation was left to state rules.

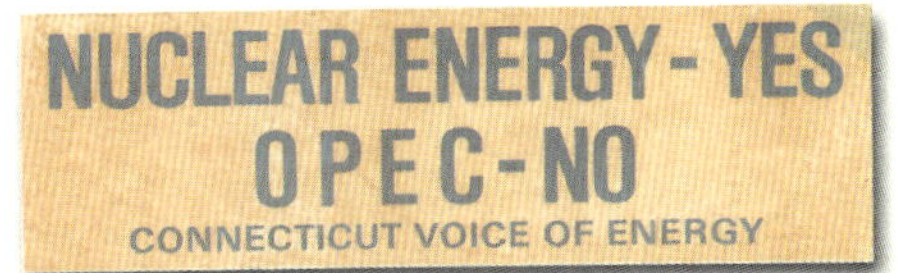

Environmental effort: floating loon nest platforms to accommodate reservoir-level changes

As the U.S. Department of Energy has noted, "This provision created, by fiat, a market in which [non-utility generators] could unilaterally sell electricity to utilities.... This is quite different from traditional regulation, which generally sets the price of electricity on the basis of the cost (to the producer) of producing it."[74]

Some states took an energetic approach to the PURPA mandate. New York, for example, passed the "6-cent law" setting that as the minimum price for non-utility power. The Maine PUC developed rules that initially involved a full-avoided-cost standard. The avoided costs were to be based on 15-year forecasts of oil and nuclear prices. As a PUC staff attorney said, "Commissioners have gone well beyond what other states have done. They deserve a pat on the back.... We will be publishing standard contracts for 15-year periods that utilities will have to accept. A dam developer just has to come in and sign up."[75] The environmental reporter who interviewed that staffer saw the implication: "Consumers would benefit from any cheap energy produced by the utilities, but most of the new hydroelectric development isn't by utilities.... For the first time, there is a possibility of windfall profits..."[76]

Repairing rate-case damage: featuring real Maine shareholders in image ads

As early as May 1981, CMP attorneys asked the PUC to reconsider its "Chapter 36" rules, warning that "rigid use of contracting" risked creating "higher-than-required costs for the electric consumer." In May 1982, President Thurlow observed that utilities always had to prove the need for higher rates, but under Maine's NUG policy, "it is ironic that a reverse burden of proof is placed on the Company to justify paying a *lower* price for electric energy."

Installing the power unit at Monty Hydro

The dispute came to a head in August 1982, when CMP sued in Superior Court for Kennebec County to stop the PUC from requiring long-term contracts at full avoided cost. As the Guy Gannett newspapers' story on the lawsuit noted, "CMP has long objected to paying avoided cost, preferring to negotiate price with power producers."[77] The attempt failed; the judge found nothing in law that blocked the PUC from making such rules. CMP continued to argue against rigid pricing based on 15-year forecasts of oil prices and hypothetical nuclear costs, and noted that negotiation was difficult if NUG owners could always fall back on the full-avoided-cost standard. But large amounts of NUG capacity were signed up on that basis. A later chairman of the Maine PUC said of the early-'80s NUG policy imposed on CMP, "Frankly, the Commission was ramming it down their throats."[78]

NUG energy taken under contract from seven small private hydro units had been about 1 percent of CMP's mix from the 1950s through the 1970s. As the PUC's promotional policy took hold, the NUG share rose to 2 percent in 1981, to 12 percent in 1985, to 30 percent in 1990, reaching a peak of 40 percent in 1993. Sources included paper-mill cogeneration (the largest suppliers), waste-to-energy plants, small hydro, wind turbines, and stand-alone biomass fired by wood waste.

Mac in 1925

Older than CMP

More than half of Maine's current residents hadn't even been born when Everett "Mac" McKenney retired from CMP in 1960 after a 46-year career.

"I went to work for them on April 20, 1914" — before the outbreak of World War I — Mac says. "I never worked for anybody else."[u]

Now 104 and CMP's oldest retiree, Mac was born in Freedom, Maine, in April 1895. He liked playing around water. "When I was a kid, I was always building a little dam in the ditch." One day, his father took him to see the Sebasticook hydroelectric plant: "I said, 'This is the job I want.'"

Mac was hired by Fred Fortier at the Messalonskee Number 2 hydro station in Oakland as a spare man for vacationing crew, and started work the same day. "When I got a job to go in that station and watch the wheels go round, I thought I had the world by the tail. I got $10.50 a week."

His education in electricity started immediately. "That first night I got scared a little bit. We had a thunder shower during the night. We got a shot of lightning that went through the meter and melted the meter half out. I said, 'Do you have this every night?'"

Mac worked at several CMP generating stations, including Bath, Belfast, Benton, Brunswick, Fairfield, and Greenville. He was on duty at Fort Halifax when he first met Walter Wyman. "I was out in the yard and I see this man come out of the barn. I had to unlock the little gate for him, so I said, 'You're big enough to jump over that fence.' It's a wonder I didn't get fired." But he learned that Wyman wasn't that kind of man. "He was all business. He never talked too much, but he was a very nice man to everybody."

Working the board in the 1920s

Bigger system, bigger board, 1970s

World War I interrupted Mac's career with Army service. He enlisted as a private in the 116th Engineer Regiment, trained as a mechanic, and was shipped to France with more than a million other American soldiers. When he returned in 1919, his job was waiting for him. Station work continued until June 1923, when Mac joined the system dispatch staff at Fort Halifax. As a dispatcher, Mac says, "My job was to have power enough on the line at the right time." That meant monitoring loads, drawing the Solon storage down at night to take the morning discharges from Wyman dam, compiling load-curve data, talking with the steam plants, taking circuits on and off-line for repair crews, and arranging water flows for the log drives that were still a big part of life on the Kennebec River, among other duties.

Dispatching was not as technology-intensive then. "In '27, when I came down from Fort Halifax to Augusta, my office was small. I had a small [system diagram] board, and what I had for equipment was a volt meter and a frequency meter and a hand-cranked adding machine."

Mac served CMP customers well for many years, working with other long-time Dispatch employees like Eugene Whittier and John Perry. By 1945, he had risen to the post of chief load dispatcher. "It was a family affair," he says of CMP in that era. "Everybody knew everybody, and it was nice."

Mac's boyhood home in Freedom had no electricity. When he moved to Waterville in 1915, "it was handy" to have lights that went on at the click of a switch. There were limits to his electric living, though. Food still went into the ice box for keeping. Like other CMP customers, Mac expanded the role of electricity in his family life, including buying a variety of Delta electric tools to pursue his woodworking hobby.

Running through a hundred years of memories that reach back to kerosene lamps and ice boxes, Mac concludes, "Electricity has changed the whole thing, and now they miss it when it's gone."

Mac with David Flanagan

Maine's NUG policy was very effective in some points: it diversified the utility energy mix, reduced reliance on imported oil, and promoted the use of renewable resources. Nor did the quality of electric service suffer: in general, NUG plants are well-engineered and operate at high standards. But the economic impacts were another matter. At their peak in 1993, NUG contracts consumed $360 million, or nearly a million dollars a day for the entire year.

CMP estimated that about two-thirds of the 50 percent run-up in its prices between 1988 and 1993 reflected the costs of adding NUGs to the mix, and often stated that some NUG contracts were priced at from two to four times competitive-market rates for energy. A 1991 Maine State Planning Office review of state policy determined that many NUG contracts embodied "prices well in excess of what would ultimately be found necessary to stimulate this alternative supply market," and added:

> These [NUG] resource commitments are one of the fundamental reasons behind today's rising rates, because they were acquired at higher than necessary prices. Unfortunately, the development of independent power may have been viewed with an excessive degree of regulatory enthusiasm, without appropriate regard to future rate impacts....we should learn to be cautious as we develop policies that look toward our energy future. [79]

CMP's energy-conservation mascot

Paper-mill power units (upper left): big sources of non-oil energy

A consulting economist examined CMP's NUG contracts compared to some NUG owners' own competitive bids in other areas and concluded that above-market pricing of NUG energy had cost Maine "about 3,700 to 4,900 jobs" — even after allowing for the increase in in-state cash circulation, employment at the NUG plants and Maine residents' gains as shareholders of some NUG-owning companies. The economist's conclusion was likely conservative: he did not attempt to quantify business-location decisions affected by the higher prices, or the costs of non-electric energy supply that looked economic only because of the NUG impacts on CMP rates.[80]

If the early years of state policy on NUGs may have reflected "too much enthusiasm and too little concern for the potential costs,"[81] it is also true that the PUC took steps to mitigate the impacts. In 1984, the PUC approved CMP's plan for the nation's first competitive request for proposals from NUG developers; prices for new contracts promptly fell below the former levels of administratively determined avoided costs. Commissioners have also supported CMP's efforts to buy out, buy down, or otherwise restructure more than 40 of the 100-plus NUG contracts it signed;[82] accepted Quebec hydro exports as an "avoided resource" to reduce benchmark avoided costs; and provided a financial incentive in ratemaking to produce more savings to share with customers. Of course, holders of the highest-priced contracts generally

Charles Monty,
Interim President, 1983-84

Aroostook Valley Electric,
Fort Fairfield: from NUG to lower-cost CMP unit as part of buyout →

have the least incentive to renegotiate. But the big, high-priced contracts of the early period have begun to lapse; when the first of these expired in October 1997, its energy was re-priced at more competitive levels, immediately saving CMP customers about $25 million a year on that one contract.

Relations with the PUC hit a low during the early '80s. Besides disputes over the Seabrook investment and NUG policy, relations were further marred in 1982 when a CMP senior vice president lied under oath to the PUC about political questions inserted by a contractor into a market-research survey on conservation-loan programs. The officer pled to a false-swearing misdemeanor and was later discharged. CMP pled guilty to a state charge of falsifying evidence in the matter and paid a $5,000 fine; it also accepted a PUC contempt finding and paid a $20,000 fine.[83] Among other casualties of this period was the 1981 proposal to create a holding company for CMP and other enterprises, to be called Maine Industries, Inc.; it was withdrawn in late 1982. Criticized for his part in the false-witness matter, Thurlow announced his early retirement in August 1983. Executive Vice President Charles E. Monty became interim president as the search for a successor proceeded.

For the first time, the CMP board of directors reached outside company ranks for a president. John W. Rowe, a 38-year-old Wisconsin native who had practiced utility law in Chicago, then served as senior vice president for legal affairs with Conrail, became president of CMP on January 9, 1984.

Rowe pledged to restore working relations with state government. He quickly added a resolve to extricate CMP from its Seabrook commitments. The challenge was to get clear of Seabrook on terms that would keep CMP solvent.

CMP had made large investments that would have to be written off if deemed imprudent and therefore ineligible for rate recovery. Boston Edison had cancelled the Pilgrim 2 nuclear project in the fall of 1981. CMP cancelled its planned Sears Island development in March 1984, and was part of a bloc representing 40 percent of Seabrook investors trying to cancel the Unit 2 project there. CMP had tried in 1983 to sell the Seabrook interest and its share of the Millstone 3 nuclear project in Connecticut, but no buyers came forward. As Rowe told shareholders at the 1984 annual meeting, the construction investments awaiting regulatory approval for recovery were equivalent to 80 percent of their equity in CMP: $69 million in Millstone 3, $180 million in Seabrook 1, $52 million in Seabrook 2, $15 million in Pilgrim, and $14 million in Sears Island. Earlier investments in the Yankee reactors

John Rowe,
President 1984-1989

Former White House economist
Alfred Kahn testifying at Maine PUC

had been "extraordinarily successful," Rowe said, saving customers more than $650 million in avoided oil purchases, but later projects had been hurt by inflation, rising interest rates, delays, and a decline in the growth of electric demand.[84]

Architect's view of expanded General Office

After Public Service Company of New Hampshire, staggering into bankruptcy, suspended construction at Seabrook in 1984, CMP and other investors took charge, canceling Unit 2 in the process. In December 1984, the Maine PUC ordered CMP and the other Maine utilities involved in Seabrook to attempt to sell their shares; in the first month of 1985, another order instructed the utilities to prepare disengagement plans. At CMP's 1985 annual meeting, Rowe pointed to CMP's "grave financial condition": the $378 million then invested in incomplete or cancelled plants exceeded CMP shareholders' entire equity investment by nearly $34 million.[85] Forced write-offs of all the expenses would obliterate the company; Bangor Hydro and Maine Public Service were in the same position.

Resolution, when it finally came, was swift. A unit of Massachusetts-based Eastern Utilities Associates agreed in early 1985 to buy CMP's Seabrook stake for $87.7 million, about 25 cents on the dollar for CMP's investment at that point. The PUC allowed gradual rate recovery of $148 million of Seabrook and $43 million of canceled-plant investments because they were deemed prudent decisions at the time they were taken (in 1979, PUC staff were urging CMP to add 8 percent to its 6 percent interest in Seabrook as an alternative to the Sears Island coal project).[86] But the Commissioners ruled that expenditures on some projects had continued past the point of reasonableness, and disallowed them. As a result, CMP took a pre-tax write-off of $85 million for Seabrook and other projects. The action led to CMP's second-quarter 1985 reporting of its first loss, but the Commission's ruling removed a mortal threat to the company's survival.

Rowe's cooperative stance toward state government took several forms. He hired an assistant attorney general, the deputy chief of the state energy office, and a PUC staff attorney. He supported new and expanded demand-side management programs. And he cultivated political support for a proposed long-term energy contract with Hydro-Quebec that could stabilize prices, or at least reduce the benchmark costs for new non-utility generation contracts.

In January 1989, the PUC rejected the proposed Hydro-Quebec contract, ruling that insufficient evidence existed to demonstrate that it satisfied Maine's new statutory preference — if other factors were equivalent — for conservation measures or cogeneration purchases over Canadian imports. At the end of the month, Rowe left CMP to run the New England Electric System holding company, whose president had been killed in an accident. Board Chairman George H. Ellis served as acting president, and Executive Vice President Matthew Hunter served as acting CEO while a nationwide search for a new president progressed.

Joe Collier, Jr.,
President 1989-1991

Joe C. Collier, Jr., took office as CMP's president and CEO on July 1, 1989. Collier had worked his way up through 30 years' service at Florida Power & Light to become a senior vice president. He reorganized management and brought extensive experience in operations and total-quality management principles to CMP. But the personal style developed in a much larger organization with different concerns, operating in a completely different regulatory and political climate, did not translate well to Collier's new post in Maine. The CMP board of directors suggested he leave. After negotiations with the board, Collier resigned on March 29, 1991. The news release negotiated with the CMP board had said Collier resigned "to pursue other opportunities." He accepted a $500,000 severance payment, required by his contract, that attracted considerable public and media comment when published in a proxy statement.

Matthew Hunter,
President 1991-1993

This time the board looked within CMP's own officer ranks and elected Matt Hunter as president and CEO. Since starting as a lineman in 1952, Hunter had worked in a wide variety of departments in both staff and supervisory capacities, giving him both breadth and depth of experience. He stepped in at a difficult time, however. A sharp recession in 1990-91 contributed to CMP's first kilowatt-hour sales decrease since 1949. A cost-cutting campaign closed three oil-fired generators at Mason Station, trimmed operating budgets, and reduced the workforce through 204 early retirements and 23 position cuts. A $55 million non-fuel rate case was withdrawn, but other increases raised overall rates 14 percent in 1991, and a December redesign of rates by the PUC drew cries of outrage from thousands of customers whose individual bills increased as a result.

David Flanagan,
President, 1994-1998
President, CMP Group, 1998-

In that setting, CMP's March 1, 1993, filing of a $95 million rate request that would hike rates another 11.7 percent encountered bitter opposition. The steep increases of the preceding three years had all been for fuel and purchased power — pass-through items on which CMP earned no profit — but the proposed new increase struck a nerve. Thousands of customers protested by letter or in comments at PUC public hearings. Some wore anti-CMP buttons and brandished placards.

CMP adjusted its request to $83 million during the year, but the PUC's final ruling in December 1993 rejected $57 million of that amount, including about $20 million that supposedly could have been saved by more efficient operations. Credit ratings promptly fell and the board cut the quarterly common-stock dividend by 42 percent.

The board elected Senior Vice President David T. Flanagan as president effective January 1, 1994, while Hunter assumed the title "chairman of the company" until his planned retirement in May. Flanagan was one of John Rowe's 1984 hires from state government. He had been an assistant Maine attorney general, a partner in a Portland law firm, and legal advisor to Governor Joseph E. Brennan. He moved into the president's office with legal and regulatory experience, good connections in government, and a mandate for change.

Protest button from 1993
rate-case public hearings

Monty Hydro, Lewiston →

A long gauntlet of difficulties dominated this 20-year period for CMP, but it did not entirely lack advances. New technologies and improved processes improved workplace safety and environmental compliance; progress included adding new environmental staff and licensing the state's only hazardous-waste handling facility to deal with transformer oil and other substances. Energy audits and other efficiency programs benefited thousands of customers. New hydro units came on-line on the Androscoggin River at Brunswick and Lewiston. Regulatory support allowed mitigating some of the cost impacts of the early NUG contracts, and the integration of non-utility sources and demand-side-management programs into competitive resource acquisition. Automated controls improved substation and power-line reliability, while a new, computerized Customer Service System allowed faster and more accurate access to account information.

Still, a residential customer's bill for 500 kilowatt-hours had climbed from \$33.34 in January 1982 to \$58.02 as of January 1994 — a 74 percent jump that well outpaced the 55 percent gain in the Consumer Price Index, and ran completely opposite the long trend of stable or declining prices. Though not the highest in New England, CMP's typical bills were no longer the lowest among major utilities. Besides creating political and regulatory difficulties, CMP's rate increases and the expectations that more would follow were creating hardships, suppressing demand, and promoting fuel switching. Even customers who accepted the evidence that most of the increase was the cost of following state policy on NUG energy could reasonably say that too much was enough.

Something had to change.

Mobile data terminal: whisking work orders wirelessly from office to truck

The Transformation

Moving past the collapse of the 1993 rate case required adjusting CMP budgets and customers' expectations. In addition to cutting the common-stock dividend, the CMP board approved a $22 million cut in the operating budget. Preparations began for reducing the workforce by at least 225 positions.

The company also moved to change customers' expectations on prices. On January 11, 1994, Flanagan held a press conference in Portland to announce, "Our goal is that in the year 2000, our customers' rates overall, adjusted for inflation, will be lower than they are today."[87] He proposed to maintain real-price stability by reducing CMP's internal costs, seeking new reductions in NUG expenses, and cooperating with regulators on competitive new products and pricing to build or maintain load. Other adjustments at this time included reducing the number of vice presidents from 12 to five, creating a marketing department, and — in a short-lived experiment widely criticized by customers — reading meters every other month and estimating the intervening bills.

smart *power*™

CMP marketing tagline, 1990s

Meanwhile, CMP's desire to change customers' expectations on rates was running parallel with PUC Chairman Thomas L. Welch's interest in reforming regulation. As a former telephone-utility lawyer and chief deputy attorney general of Pennsylvania, he had been involved in devising performance-based regulation that combined indexed price caps and performance adjustments for

← Overleaf: Renewal — good for circuits, and for companies

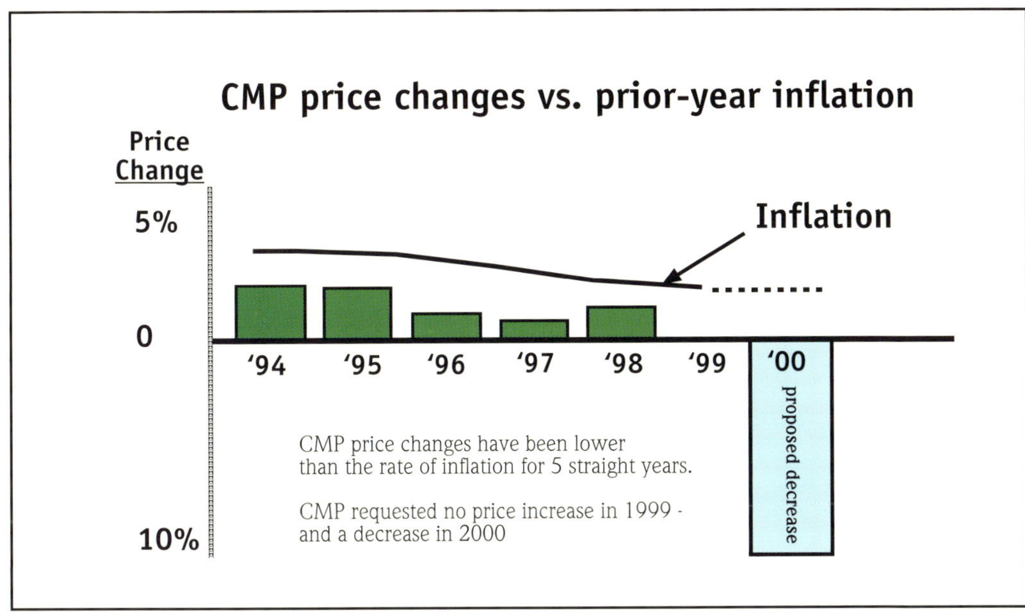

← Showing customers the effects of the ARP price caps, with asset-sale cut proposed for 2000

telecommunications companies. After more than a year of investigation and negotiations, PUC staff, CMP, the Office of the Public Advocate, and other parties agreed on the country's first indexed price-cap system for an electric utility. With PUC approval, the Alternative Rate Plan or ARP took effect January 1, 1995.

The mayors of Safety City, traveling educational demo

The ARP replaced the annual "fuel-clause" proceeding for changes in fuel and purchased-power costs, and utility-initiated "base-rate" filings for other costs. The traditional system typically involved months of litigation, enormous amounts of time and paperwork for participants, and rates that could change several times a year in ways that customers could not predict.

By contrast, the ARP called for a one adjustment to rate caps each July. The formula started with the prior-year change in the federal Gross Domestic Product Price Index. It subtracted a fixed "productivity offset," then adjusted the result depending on CMP's performance on several service indicators. A sharing provision would allow rate changes to reflect half of the excess or deficiency in CMP's profitably outside a defined band to protect the company and customers. The PUC also retained authority to consider extraordinary events like weather catastrophes that were not reflected in basic rates or price indices. For its part, CMP had discretion to refrain from using all of a permitted adjustment if competitive factors weighed against the increase.

Internet debut of http://www.cmpco.com May 22, 1996

Uranium fuel pellets

The ARP achieved its intended results. The formula-driven price-cap adjustments were 2.43 percent in 1995, 1.26 percent in 1996, 1.1 percent in 1997, 1.33 percent in 1998, and zero in 1999. In every case, the change was less than the prior-year inflation rate: the real price of CMP electricity was falling. At the same time, CMP used its pricing flexibility with PUC support to devise special rates and contracts to avoid load loss that might increase price pressure for remaining customers. New rates helped retain electric water heaters, ski resorts' snow-making equipment, and utility power at lumber mills and other businesses that might be tempted to install diesel self-generation.

Sensitivity to cost risks helped close an era for CMP in 1997. The Maine Yankee nuclear plant had been off-line since December 6, 1996. An extensive program of inserting alloy sleeves into thousands of tubes in the plant's steam generators had proven economic, but other difficulties demanded attention. Safety concerns were raised about electric-cable separation in the control systems, and evidence developed of fuel-rod leaks. Following the December 1996 shutdown, the Nuclear Regulatory Commission told Maine Yankee Atomic Power Company management that the plant could not restart without explicit NRC approval. For the first time, Maine Yankee was on the NRC "watch list" of "troubled plants."

Maine Yankee fuel-rod assembly →

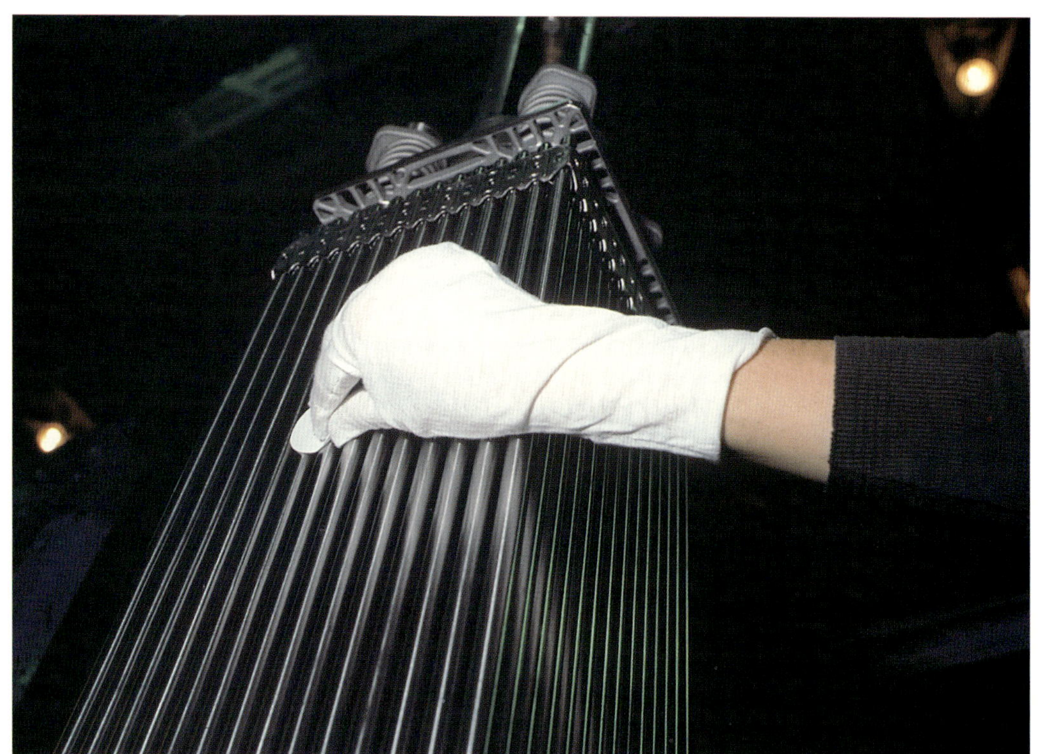

Technicians and consultants ran computer scenarios that strongly suggested further repairs were unlikely to be worthwhile even if the plant ran well through its remaining license term in 2008. On August 6, 1997, Flanagan and other CMP representatives on the Maine Yankee board joined in a unanimous vote to close the plant permanently and commence the decommissioning process.

Maine Yankee's last years and the closing decision were difficult, but the plant's nearly 24 years of operation were a boon for CMP customers. Between January 1973 and December 1996, Maine Yankee produced 118.7 billion kilowatt-hours of energy at an average cost of 2.5 cents per kilowatt-hour.[88] CMP's 38 percent share of that energy typically supplied a fifth of the kilowatt-hours sold to CMP customers.

Compared to the second-choice, late-'60s CMP alternative of another oil-fired plant, Maine Yankee saved CMP customers at least $1 billion in terms of 1997 purchasing power, even after making generous allowances for decommissioning and waste-disposal costs.[89] In any case, the closing of CMP's largest single source of energy was merely a foretaste of changes to come.

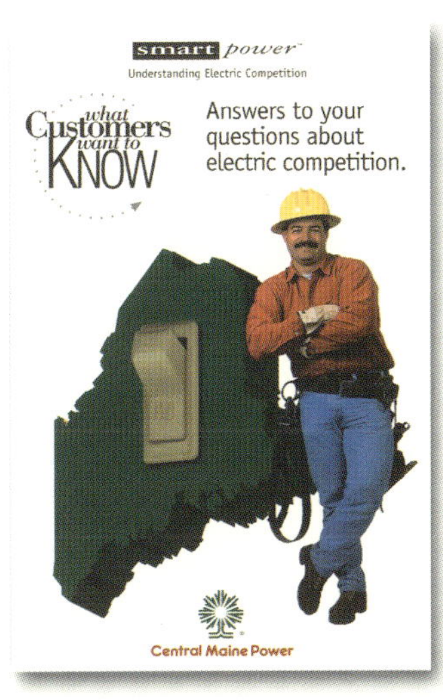

← Spent-fuel pool, Maine Yankee

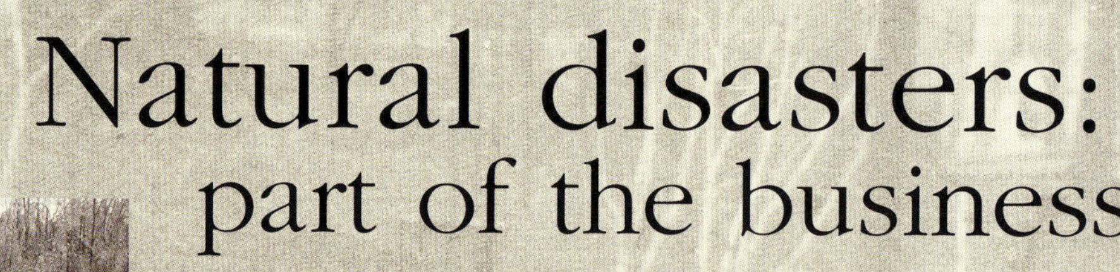

Natural disasters: part of the business

Maine's many repeat visitors include natural disasters.

Maine lies halfway between the Equator and the Arctic Circle, exposed to summer air from the southwest and to winter blasts from the Canadian Shield, so it enjoys both heavy rains and heavy snows. It has hundreds of streams and six river systems exceeding 100 miles in length, so it is subject to floods. The state abuts the Atlantic Ocean, so it is exposed to fierce nor'easters and to hurricanes. It is the nation's most heavily forested state — trees cover 90 percent of its land surface — so winds and ice storms can wreak havoc as limbs and trees fall on power lines.

With 2,300 miles of overhead transmission line and nearly 20,000 miles of overhead distribution line, CMP has big stakes on the table whenever disaster strikes. (Its 1,400 miles of underground and submarine cable face their own operating risks, but they are usually not weather-related.)

The biggest natural disaster to strike the CMP system — and probably the state itself, in recorded history at least — was the great ice storm that struck upstate New York, northern New England, and Quebec in January 1998.[v] It began in Maine as a freezing drizzle on January 5, then on January 7 turned into a 50-hour bout of freezing rain that coated exposed surfaces with up to 3 inches of ice. Limbs bent and broke. Trees leaned and fell, breaking utility poles as they dropped. Lines sagged, ripping service connections from the sides of buildings and sometimes pulling poles over by sheer weight. It was even worse in Quebec, where whole lines of transmission towers crumpled under more than foot-thick coatings of ice. But it was bad enough in Maine.

By January 9, about 275,000 of CMP's 520,000 customer accounts were out of service. Continuing bad weather took some circuits out several times, so the total of customer-outage reports in the first few days approached 340,000. A smaller storm on January 24 inflicted another 75,000 outages. Governor King proclaimed a state of emergency and called out the National Guard. The President of the United States declared 15 of Maine's 16 counties a federal disaster area.

Mounting an all-out restoration effort, CMP brought in more than 2,000 utility and contract line-crew members and tree crews from as far away as Nova Scotia and Michigan. Military transport planes airlifted crews and equipment from the Carolinas. Merchants donated cold-weather gear and other supplies, but CMP still spent more than $50 million on storm restoration, including the costs of replacing 3,000 broken poles and 1,500 transformers. The last year-round customer was restored on January 30; some seasonal buildings blocked by fallen trees or broken poles weren't cleared until April.

Ice Storm '98 was the most spectacular disaster to befall CMP, but far from the only one. A smaller but still-vicious ice storm hit the Portland area and central Maine in the winter of 1929. For warmer weather ordeals, Hurricane Bob in 1991 and Hurricane Gloria in 1985 caused 400,000 outages between them. The year 1954 saw Hurricane Carol strike on August 31, followed by Hurricane Edna on September 11, knocking out power for half of CMP's 200,000 customers and requiring 1,200 pole replacements among other repairs.

Hurricanes may compare well to ice storms, however: warmer temperatures and bare ground usually mean less outage discomfort for customers and better working conditions for repair crews. Hurricane Gloria, for example, caused nearly 250,000 outages, but 80 percent of them were restored by the end of the next day.

Brunswick power house in 1936 floods

Floods also come with the territory. Widespread flooding was particularly destructive in the spring of 1936. CMP's Brunswick Station flooded twice to the tops of its windows. The generators at Shawmut hydro were under water, and a six-ton generator at Unions Fall on the Saco River was pushed off its foundation. Substations flooded out; Bath was out of power for days. Fred Clement of the West Buxton hydro station cheerfully worked from the roof, using a crowbar on a rope to break windows and ease the flood waters' pressure against the building. He said he had always wanted to get paid for breaking windows. [w]

Severe flooding struck again in 1987, when the Kennebec overtopped the Route 201 bridge in Skowhegan. Some substations were disconnected as a precaution against rising waters, as were thousands of customers' premises.

Careful design specifications, systematic tree trimming and vegetation control, and prompt dispatch of repair crews help prevent outages and mitigate their impact. But some disasters originate far away. Sun-spot activity 93 million miles distant can disrupt power flows and electrical equipment. Whether the instrument is a tree limb or a solar flare, whether the year is 1899 or 1999, natural forces pose a continuing threat to steady electric service.

The proliferation of NUG plants and a 1992 federal law mandating open access to utility transmission lines at posted, non-discriminatory prices had greatly stimulated competition in wholesale energy markets — federally regulated transactions among utilities and non-utility wholesale generators. Alert to the possibility that retail competition might deliver savings for consumers and enhance business climates, a growing number of state commissions and legislatures began studying utility restructuring. California, Massachusetts, New York, and Pennsylvania moved early in this trend.

The electric Zamboni takes to the ice, North Yarmouth Academy

Maine took steps as well. The Legislature directed the PUC to produce a study and draft legislation. On May 29, 1997, Governor Angus S. King signed "An Act to Restructure the State's Electric Industry."[90]

The new law decreed that customers of investor-owned Maine electric utilities would be able to choose their electric-energy supplier as of March 1, 2000. Competitive suppliers would be licensed and monitored by the PUC, but their prices would be unregulated. Customers who made no selection would default to a "standard offer" service arranged by the PUC after competitive bidding.

To promote a competitive supply market, the state required CMP, Bangor Hydro, and Maine Public Service to sell their non-nuclear generating assets, including the energy taken under NUG contracts. The utilities' responsibility to supply energy would end as of March 1, 2000. At that time, they could sell electricity through an affiliate, but CMP and Bangor Hydro affiliates would be limited to 33 percent of the kilowatt-hours sold in their own service territory. The utilities would remain responsible for operating, maintaining, and repairing substations and power lines, and performing related customer services. The PUC would design new utility rates to strip out energy charges, and include only the costs of energy delivery plus approved generation-related costs incurred under traditional regulation that would otherwise be "stranded" and uncollectible after the transition.

Jim Wright, known for safety broadcasts ending 'No line is safe to touch — evah'

CMP acted swiftly to comply with the law. Even before the measure took final form, Flanagan told a legislative committee on April 28, 1997, that CMP would soon test the market for its generation assets. Strong interest in the

New England Electric System auction suggested good prices could be had. A rigorous competitive-bidding process began in June; final bids were taken from a variety of U.S. and foreign parties on December 10, 1997.

The first CMP Group annual report

Following final negotiations on a sale agreement, Flanagan joined an officer from the winning bidder's organization on January 6, 1998, to announce that Florida-based FPL Group would pay $846.5 million for 1,185 megawatts of CMP generation: 31 hydroelectric facilities, three oil-fired stations, and an Aroostook County wood-fired plant acquired via a NUG-contract restructuring. The price — proportionately much better than NEES or Boston Edison obtained for their assets — was far above the units' net accounting value of some $230 million, offering an opportunity to deliver a significant rate reduction by using the above-book value to pay off large amounts of authorized-but-unrecovered costs, reducing CMP's future revenue requirements.

Preparations for closing the sale were well advanced when FPL Energy, the unit actually slated to take possession, filed suit in a New York City federal court in November to kill the deal. FPL Energy claimed pending changes in federal rules on transmission access in New England had substantially reduced the value of the CMP assets, triggering the sales agreement's "material adverse event" clause. CMP contested the claim, noting among other things that FPL Energy knew from studying the NEES auction that federal rules could change. CMP's position was supported in a joint friend-of-the-court brief from Maine's Attorney General, PUC, and Public Advocate.

Michael Yackira, FPL Energy, and David Flanagan closing power-plant sale, April 1999

Less than three hours into the trial on March 11, 1999, the judge ruled from the bench that FPL Energy must carry out its obligations. No appeal was made, and the sale was completed with a ceremonial signing in Portland on April 7, with Governor King as guest of honor. After payments for ancillary property, fuel, and inventories were added to the original price, a total of $858.3 million was wired into CMP accounts. Much of the cash proceeds was already spoken for: state and federal taxes would consume $300 million, mortgage-bond redemptions would use $120 million, a temporary energy buy-back would use about $100 million. Remaining cash could be used to redeem more debt, reduce stock liabilities, or reinvest in the business — all without impeding regulators' ability to offset stranded costs by the amount of the surplus accounting value. At the same time, more than 200 CMP generation-related employees transferred to FPL Energy, ending a 99-year tradition of CMP-owned generation.

Among the sold: Harris Station, upper Kennebec — CMP's biggest hydro plant →

Many other steps remained to be taken to prepare for March 1, 2000. A big one would be the sale of the energy from renewable-resource or cogeneration NUG projects, from CMP's small interests in the Vermont Yankee and Millstone 3 nuclear plants, and from a regional transmission link with Quebec. The price for this 3 billion-plus kilowatt-hour energy stream would help the PUC determine the level of stranded costs to be recovered in CMP's energy-delivery rates in the first few years after retail competition began.

Another key step to deal with competition and change was creation of the CMP Group holding company on September 1, 1998. A new president directed operations: Flanagan stepped up to the helm of CMP Group, while human-resources executive Sara J. Burns became CMP's first woman president. A new vision guided the company: "to be the premier rural transmission and distribution utility."

Union Water Power

The change, approved by shareholders and federal and state regulators, made CMP the principal holding of CMP Group, but also set up several former CMP units as independent, unregulated businesses. They included MainePower, a unit preparing to operate as a competitive electricity marketer; Union Water-Power, whose business included river-facilities management, utility support services, and real estate; CNEX, which provided domestic and international consulting and research; New England Gas Development, which held CMP's investment in the CMP Natural Gas venture; MaineCom Services, which invested in fiber-optic capacity for communications carriers in the Northeast and held a 38 percent share of NorthEast Optic Network, a Portland-to-New York City fiber system; and TeleSmart, an accounts-receivable management service for several large utilities.

Sara Burns,
President since 1998

MainePower did not survive the year. CMP Group concluded that the prospects for a market-limited reseller of electricity facing large, less rule-bound competitors did not justify further development. The subsidiary was closed at year-end. But the other unregulated subsidiaries continued to seek new business and develop new offerings as part of a broad-based growth strategy.

Similar considerations about size and competitiveness led the CMP Group board early in 1999 to authorize exploration of opportunities to combine with another company. Central Maine Power accounted for more than 95 percent of CMP Group's revenues, but as a non-generating "wires" company, it would face the business risk of recovering its costs through kilowatt-hour charges. There would be little margin for error, and state law forbade recovering system costs from large customers who switched fuels or left the grid to self-generate. A strong trend toward T&D company consolidation was already clear in the industry as utilities sought defensive or expansionist options.

CMP Natural Gas construction,
North Windham

Although management explored several possibilities, the most obvious potential partner was one with whom CMP already had a working relationship — a subsidiary of New York-based Energy East Corporation was CMP's partner in forming the CMP Natural Gas venture to serve 35 Maine communities that had no natural-gas distribution.

On June 15, 1999, CMP Group President David Flanagan and Energy East Chairman and President Wesley von Schack told an Augusta press conference that the two companies had signed a merger agreement. If CMP Group shareholders and several state and federal regulatory bodies approved, Energy East would redeem all outstanding shares of CMP Group common stock at $29.50, and Flanagan would become president of Energy East as well as CMP Group. Central Maine Power would remain a Maine-based company with its own management team, continuing to serve Maine customers from Augusta under the supervision of the Maine Public Utilities Commission.

David Flanagan, CMP Group, (at lectern) and Wesley von Schack, Energy East, announcing merger agreement, June 15, 1999 → (*Kennebec Journal* photo)

The final decisions on the proposed merger might not be known until the spring of the year 2000. That story runs beyond the scope of this book. But even setting aside the merger announcement, CMP had changed, dramatically and perhaps irreversibly. The beloved power plants were gone. The transmission grid was open to all comers. The workforce was smaller than it had been 50 years before.

Electricity, too, had changed. What was a novelty and a luxury 100 years earlier was now a legally recognized necessity of modern life, surging into laser disks, microwave ovens, computers, CAT scans, and other devices not even dreamed of by the two men who rented a buggy to go buy a little generator in Oakland on a November evening in 1899.

While CMP prepared itself for a new business environment and a second century of service, one thing remained constant: the determination that electricity should be distributed safely, widely, and reliably, and that whoever generated the power, the light from the river would still shine.

Main sources

Baldwin, Neil. *Edison: Inventing the Century.* New York: Hyperion, 1995. A recent biography of the great inventor, with good explanations of technologies.

Beck, Bill. *Light Across the Prairies: An Illustrated History of Northwestern Public Service Company.* Eden Prairie, Minn.: Viking Press, 1989. A corporate history published in the centennial of South Dakota's statehood, this book has a useful treatment of the early years of electricity and the operations of Samuel Insull's Middle West Utilities holding company, of which Northwestern Public Service, like CMP, was once a part.

Boorstin, Daniel J. *The Americans: The Democratic Experience.* New York: Random House, 1973. Chapter 56, "The Social Inventor: Inventing for the Market," describes Edison's marketing of electric lighting.

Central Maine Power Company. Annual Reports to Shareholders, 1930 et seq. Corporate annual reports are subject to SEC regulations and the examination of independent auditors, and are a definitive source of basic statistics. In recent years, requirements for "management discussion and analysis" in the report or the annual-meeting proxy provide another formal record of key events and issues.

Central Maine Power Company. *The Exciter.* Company monthly newsletter (named for the electrical start-up device on a generator) published 1918-1922, primarily as a preferred-stock sales campaign promotional medium, then revived in 1925 as a broader-purpose newsletter. Published until 1979. Items range from Walter Wyman's 1925 discussion of the sale of CMP to the Insull operation, to an October 1947 note that the former Lena May Beal of the Portland Machine Room billing operation had a new son. Special issues include a useful 1960 production on CMP's trolley lines, and the November 1974 issue, "CMP's 75th Anniversary." Newsletter articles are inherently less structured and more promotional than formal financial reports, but they do receive internal review and can often provide valuable, if sometimes unintended, insight into the workings of a business and the lives of its employees.

Central Maine Power Company. *Employee Update*, later *Weekly Update.* The current Company newsletter, started in August 1977.

Hegarty, George D. "Central Maine Power Company." Unpublished typescript, 50 pp., ca. 1948. Hegarty, born in Winthrop in 1880 and schooled, like Walter Wyman and Harvey Eaton, at Coburn Classical Institute, joined the Company in 1903 as Walter Wyman's assistant, was Clerk from 1906, and later manager of CMP's Northern Division operations based in Waterville. He was a member of the original CMP board of directors elected in 1910. His narrative is an unadorned but informative story of the early years of CMP with some details of his work with Wyman. Copy in CMP archives.

Heppenheimer, T.A. "American Prometheus." *Audacity: The Magazine of Business Experience.* 2:4 (Summer 1994). A useful summary of Samuel Insull's role in the U.S. electric-utility industry.

Hormell, Orren C., Ph.D. "Maine's Public Utilities." Brunswick, Maine: Bowdoin College Bulletin No. 164, February 1927. Hormell's long life (1879-1976) extended from the early days of electrification to the heyday of nuclear power. His 1927 booklet offers a useful summary of the growth of utility regulation in Maine and of the CMP system. Writing before the days of the Securities & Exchange Commission and the Public Utility Holding Company Act, he was deeply skeptical of the intentions and financial stability of Middle West and other national holding companies of the 1920s.

Judd, Richard W., et al., eds. *Maine: The Pine Tree State from Prehistory to the Present.* Orono: University of Maine Press, 1995. A comprehensive view of the state from many contributors; strong on social and economic history, including the growth of CMP, the Fernald Law, and the debate over public rights in hydro development.

Libby, Herbert C. Unpublished typescript history of CMP, 158 pp., 1948. According to the March 1, 1965, obituary in the Waterville *Morning Sentinel*, Libby's father built street railways in Maine and New Brunswick. Libby was born in Burnham in 1878, studied at Colby, then took a degree in English and history at Harvard. He was a professor of English and public speaking at Colby, retiring in 1944, and had earlier served as mayor of Waterville. He wrote or edited several books. His manuscript on CMP contains passages based on personal interviews with Harvey Eaton, and bears reviewers' annotations by CMP chairman William Skelton and vice president George Williams. Copy in CMP archives.

McGuire, Patrick, and Granovetter, Mark. "Shifting Boundaries and Social Construction in the Early Electricity Industry, 1878-1915." Two sociologists review the motivations and interactions of public and private interests, explaining why personages on both sides sought regulation. Posted on the University of Toledo Internet site, http://sasweb.utoledo.edu/sasw/PORACVEN.htm, 1998, accessed April 27, 1999.

National Museum of American History, The Smithsonian Institution, Washington, D.C. "Powering the Past: A Look Back." Internet pages on the history of the U.S. electric industry. http://www.si.edu/organiza/museums/nmah/csr/powering/thepast.htm Updated November 1998; accessed May 1, 1999.

Nye, David E. *Electrifying America: Social Meanings of a New Technology.* Cambridge, Mass.: MIT, 1990. A wide-ranging view of pre-electric America and the transformations wrought by electric light and power.

Rolde, Neil. *Maine: A Narrative History.* Gardiner, Maine: Tilbury House, 1990. A compact, gracefully written overview with many well-wrought vignettes, as on Governor Percival Baxter and his beloved 14 dogs.

Skelton, William B. "Walter S. Wyman (1874-1942)—One of Maine's Great Pioneers." New York: The Newcomen Society in North America, 1949. 32 pp. An address by CMP Chairman and former President Skelton, a long-time associate of Wyman, at the 1949 Maine Luncheon of the Newcomen Society of England, held at The Augusta House, Augusta, Maine, September 29, 1949. The rhetoric is in the heroic mode, but Skelton offers a good summary of CMP's development and a colleague's view of Wyman's thinking.

Notes

1 Oakland Area Historical Society, "Industry," Internet document at http://members.mint.net/mdenis/oahs/Industry.html, posted July 1998 by Michael Denis, accessed 25 February 1999.

2 Jean Gimpel, *The Medieval Machine: The Industrial Revolution of the Middle Ages* (New York: Holt, 1976), p. 3.

3 Hegarty, p. 4.

4 McGuire.

5 National Museum of American History.

6 CMP *Exciter*, August 1960, p. 6.

7 Libby, pp. 5-6.

8 National Museum of American History.

9 Nye, xiii.

10 Nye, pp. 235-236.

11 Nye, p. 242.

12 "Historic Consumer Price Index, 1800-1998," University of Michigan Documents Center, posted on the Internet at http://henry.ugl.lib.umich.edu/libhome/Documents.center/historiccpi.html, accessed May 25, 1999.

13 Nye, p. 260.

14 Skelton, p. 10.

15 Libby, p. 26.

16 Libby, p. 28.

17 Hegarty, pp. 14-15.

18 Libby, p. 34.

19 Hegarty, p. 15.

20 Typescript prospectus for 6% cumulative preferred stock, 1909, p. 5, CMP archives.

21 Messalonskee Electric Company, "Charter Rights and Public Franchises," typescript signed by Harvey Eaton, undated yet datable by its references to events of 1909 and the introduction of the name Central Maine Power in 1910. Copy in CMP archives.

22 Rolde, p. 298.

23 Carbon copy of letter to Delmont Emerson, pp. 1-2, CMP archives.

24 Wyman wrote a vigorous summary of his long-standing arguments against the Fernald Law in the CMP *Exciter* of June 25, 1926, p. 5.

25 "Maine's Water Power Question," ad reprint, CMP *Exciter*, December 31, 1926, p. 4.

26 Rolde, p. 313.

27 Hegarty, p. 25.

28 Richard W. Judd, "Hydroelectric Power Development," in Judd et al., pp. 441-442.

29 National Museum of American History.

30 CMP *Exciter*, Oct. 9, 1920, p. 4.

31 As Maine's highest court has said, "A public utility yields to the sovereign [the state] with respect to approval of rates, methods of financing and other matters of policy which are ordinarily within the sole province of management in private business. In return for relinquishing the right to determine without let or hindrance whom it will serve, what it will charge, or how it will finance or invest, it is usually given relative freedom from competition in its service area on the part of the public utilities similarly regulated and controlled. The monopoly thus afforded as among competing public utilities is in effect a quid pro quo for the obligation to render public service and to submit to regulation and control." — Maine Supreme Judicial Court, *Dickinson v. Maine Public Service Co.*, 223 A.2d 435, 438 (Me. 1966).

32 Hegarty, p. 44.

33 CMP *Exciter*, Dec. 25, 1920, p. 1.

34 Skelton, pp. 14-15.

35 CMP *Exciter*, in answer to employee question, March 25, 1927.

36 Skelton, p. 15.

37 Hegarty's typescript history of the company through 1948 is conspicuously silent about the arrival of Middle West Utilities officials in Maine. Another CMP chronicler, Herbert Libby, delicately recorded the MWU collapse in one sentence: "The year 1932 saw the withdrawal from the Board of Mr. Insull." (Libby, p. 48.)

38 MWU Systems map of 1930, in Beck, p. 60.

39 Letter to stockholders, CMP *Exciter*, Aug. 28, 1925, p. 1.

40 Skelton, p. 16.

41 CMP *Exciter*, July 29, 1928, pp. 1-2.

42 Hegarty, p. 21.

43 "Tractors, Truck-Tractors, and Trucks Make 2,500,000-Yd. Earth Fill at Wyman Dam," *Construction Methods*, February 1931, p. 34.

44 CMP *Exciter*, July 29, 1928, p. 1.

45 CMP *Exciter*, April 24, 1931, p. 1.

46 Paul Johnson, *A History of the American People* (New York: HarperCollins, 1997), pp. 733ff.

47 CMP *Exciter*, Jan. 30, 1931, p. 1.

48 National Electric Light Association report cited in CMP *Exciter*, Sept. 26, 1930, p. 8.

49 Orren Chalmer Hormell, "Maine Public Utilities" (Brunswick, Maine: Bowdoin College Bulletin No. 164), February 1927, p.21.

50 Richard H. Condon et al., "Maine in Depression and War, 1929-1945," in Judd et al., pp. 515-516.

51 CMP *Exciter*, July 1938, p. 2.

52 CMP *Exciter*, July 1939, p. 6.

53 Skelton, p. 21.

54 Editorials reprinted in the CMP *Exciter*, November 1942, p. 3.

55 March 1942, p. 4.

56 CMP *Exciter*, September 1942, p. 2.

57 CMP *Exciter*, May 1947, p. 14.

58 CMP *Exciter*, June 1947, p. 6.

59 CMP *Exciter*, December 1947, pp. 1, 8.

60 Noted in remarks by Executive Vice President Charles Monty at the dedication of Monty Station in Lewiston, CMP *Employee Update*, August 19, 1987, p. 1.

61 "Other Concerns Are Likely to Follow GM In Splitting Posts of Chairman and CEO," November 4, 1992, p. B1. The article featured CMP in a sidebar, complete with drawings of then Chairman Carlton D. Reed and President Matthew Hunter, as an early example of the outside-chairman arrangement.

62 CMP *Exciter*, February 1969, p. 8.

63 "The Great Northeast Blackout of 1965," based on a presentation by CMP engineer David Conroy to the Maine Section of IEEE, posted on the Internet at http://www.cmpco.com/aboutCMP/powersystem/blackout.html, updated May 19, 1997, accessed May 23, 1999.

64 According to the U.S. Energy Information Administration, the average size of thermal electric plants doubled between 1960 and 1970, but the British Thermal Units of energy they consumed to produce a kilowatt-hour of electricity (their "heat rate") fell only marginally, from 10,800 to 10,500 BTU. "Thermal-Electric Plant Construction Cost and Annual Production Expenses—1979," (Washington, D.C., May 1982), p. 10.

65 CMP *Exciter*, June 1971, p. 3.
66 CMP *Exciter*, June 1973, p. 3.
67 James L. Williams, "Oil Price History and Analysis" (London, Arkansas: WTRG Economics, 1999), an Internet document posted at http://www.wtrg.com/prices.htm, accessed May 28, 1999.
68 CMP *Exciter*, April 1975, p. 3.
69 CMP *Exciter*, November 1975, p. 2.
70 CMP *Exciter*, December 1976, pp. 7, 10.
71 CMP *Employee Update*, July 19, 1978, p. 2.
72 The U.S. Nuclear Regulatory Commission, which faulted owner General Public Utilities' conduct during the TMI accident and imposed new safety rules on all nuclear plants in the aftermath, nonetheless says flatly that TMI involved "only very small off-site releases of radioactivity" and "led to no deaths or injuries to plant workers or members of the nearby community." See "Three Mile Island 2 Accident," an NRC Internet document posted at http://www.nrc.gov/OPA/gmo/tip/tmi.htm, accessed June 3, 1999.
73 Comments of CMP President Thurlow, reported in the *Update*, October 1, 1980, p. 1.
74 Energy Information Administration, DOE, "The Changing Structure of the Electric Industry: Federal Legislative Impacts," Internet document posted at http://www.eia.doe.gov/cneaf/electricity/chg_str/chapter4.html. Last modified May 30, 1997, accessed May 25, 1999.
75 David Moskovitz, later a PUC commissioner himself and then a consultant in "least-cost planning," quoted in Robert C. Cummings, "Hydro Power," *Maine Sunday Telegram*, May 24, 1981, p. 3D.
76 Robert C. Cummings, "Hydro Power," *Maine Sunday Telegram*, May 24, 1981, p. 1.
77 Charles W. Goldsmith, "Central Maine Power sues PUC over cogeneration," Waterville *Morning Sentinel*, August 11, 1982, p. 8.
78 Kenneth Gordon, Ph.D., oral deliberations in Maine PUC Docket 92-233, October 6, 1992.
79 Richard Silkman and John Flumerfelt, "Planning Maine's Energy Future," *Maine Policy Review* 1:1 (University of Maine, December 1991), pp. 52-53, 59.
80 Ralph E. Townsend, Ph.D., "Impact of NUG Power Costs upon CMP Customers and the Maine Economy," research monograph prepared for CMP, March 7, 1994, p. 1.
81 Comments of John M. Flumerfelt, Director of Energy Policy and Planning, Maine State Planning Office, before the Joint Standing Committee on Utilities, Maine Legislature, August 27, 1992, pp. 4-5.
82 These cost-mitigation efforts, directed by CMP's Arthur Adelberg, Frederick Woodruff, and Edward Chaisson, are estimated to have saved CMP customers the net-present-value equivalent of at least $500 million compared to the original contract terms.
83 The recitation of events is based on the "Memorandum and Order" filed in Docket Civil 85-0187-B by the Office of the Clerk, United States District Court, Bangor, Maine, October 23, 1989, pp. 4-13.
84 CMP *Update*, May 23, 1984, p. 1.
85 CMP *Update*, May 22, 1985, p. 1.
86 The *Kennebec Journal* noted the earlier position of PUC staff in an editorial reprinted in CMP's *Update* May 8, 1985, pp. 1-2.
87 CMP *Update*, January 12, 1994, p. 1.
88 MYAPCo testimony in FERC Docket ER98-570-000, November 5, 1997, p. 3.
89 Based on calculations by staff of CMP's Energy Trading and Marketing Department, using construction- and operating-cost data for similar-sized oil plants and historic price data for fuel oil, summarized in a September 1998 white paper prepared by CMP Corporate Communications, "Was Maine Yankee good for CMP customers?" The paper notes that savings might have been larger if additional NUG energy at prices governed by early-'80s policies displaced some or all of the hypothetical oil-fired energy supply.
90 Chapter 32 of Title 35-A of Maine's revised statutes, also posted on the PUC Internet site at http://www.state.me.us/mpuc/Idl804.pdf,

Sidebar Notes

a Hegarty.
b CMP *Exciter*, Oct-Nov 1953, pp. 1, 4.
c Electronic correspondence from Arthur T. Eaton (b. 1923), seventh of Harvey Eaton's eight children, received at CMP on May 7, 1999. "During my growing-up years," Arthur Eaton says, "Father rarely talked about matters related to CMP. Most of my knowledge of his career with the company came from my mother. He did relate a few stories to me after I returned to Waterville and joined him in the practice of law in 1950."
d Jim McClay, Jr., "Around the Town," Waterville *Morning Sentinel*, October 20, 1953.
e CMP *Exciter*, November 1942, p. 2.
f The information on Maine trolley companies is drawn largely from a special issue of the CMP *Exciter* 42 (1960).
g Nye, 85 ff.
h Nye, 85ff.

i Nye, p. 16.
j CMP *Exciter*, Feb. 26, 1926, p. 5.
k CMP *Exciter*, May 28, 1926, pp. 1, 8.
l CMP *Exciter*, April 24, 1925, p. 4.
m Heppenheimer, p. 30.
n Heppenheimer, p. 35.
o Heppenheimer, p. 37.
p National Museum of American History.
q Beck, p. 46.
r CMP *Exciter*, May 27, 1927, pp. 1, 8.
s CMP *Exciter*, November 1937, p. 3.
t This and her other reminiscences appear in "Alice Sweetland: CMP's First Girl Meter Reader," CMP *Exciter*, June 1975, p. 7.
u Remarks transcribed from videotaped oral-history interview with Everett A. McKenney conducted by CMP Corporate Communications in April 1999.
v Ice Storm '98 data are summarized in Ice Storm '98: A CMP Photographic Journal (Augusta, Maine: CMP Corporate Communications, 1998), a commemorative book whose net proceeds go to the Maine United Way Storm Relief Fund.
w CMP *Exciter*, March 1946, p. 7.

CMP business family tree

Year to CMP	Year to Predecessor	
1899		Oakland Electric Light Co. sold to Wyman and Eaton, who reincorporate as Oakland Electric Co.
1901		Messalonskee Electric Co. organized for Waterville operations.
1905		Messalonskee's charter expanded, Oakland Electric absorbed.
1910		Name changed to Central Maine Power Co.
1910		Sebasticook Power Company
	1905	Pittsfield Electric Company
1910		Sebasticook Water Power Company
1910		Fort Halifax Power Company
1911		Kennebec Light & Heat Company
	1887	Augusta Gas Light Company
	1867	Augusta & Hallowell Gas Light Co. (name change)
	1888	Gardiner Gas Light Company
	1888	Hallowell Gas Light Company
1911		Bingham Electric Company
1911		Dexter Electric Company
1911		Skowhegan Electric Light Company
1911		Vassalborough Electric Light & Power Co.
1911		Waterville & Fairfield Railway & Light Co.
	1892	Waterville & Fairfield Railroad Co.
	1892	Waterville Electric Light & Power Co.
	1892	Fairfield Electric Light Company
1911		Union Gas & Electric Company
1912		Clinton Electric Light & Power Company
1911		Corinna Plant (Ireland Bros.) (Dist. Plant Only)
1912		Richmond Light Company
1912		Canaan Power Company
1914		Skowhegan Electric Company
1918		Bombazee Power Company
1920		Solon Electric Company
1920		Penobscot Bay Electric Company
	1908	Bucksport Light & Power Company
	1909	Belfast Gas & Electric Company
	1913	Searsport Electric Company
	1915	Greenville Light & Power Company
	1914	Sebec Power Company
	1909	Wilson Stream Dam Company
	1914	Dover & Foxcroft Light & Heat Co.
	1914	Sangerville Improvement Company
1920		Bath & Brunswick Light & Power Company
	1910	Brunswick Electric Light & Power Company
	1910	Sagadahoc Light & Power Company
	1900	Bath Gas & Electric Company
	1890	Bath Electric Light & Power Company
	1890	Bath Gas Light Company
1920		Hartland Electric Light & Power Company
1920		Newport Light & Power Company
	1902	The Smith-Sturtevant Light & Power Co. (Name changed to Newport Light & Power Company, 1902)
1920		Union Light & Power Company
1920		Waldoboro Water & Electric Light & Power Co.
1920		Wiscasset Electric Light & Power Company
1921		Knox County Electric Company
	1919	Rockland, Thomaston & Camden Street Railway (Name changed to Knox County Electric Co., 1919)
	1891	Camden & Rockport Street Railway Co.
	1891	Thomaston Street Railway Company
	1891	Rockland Street Railway Company
	1901	Knox Gas & Electric Company
	1893	Camden & Rockport Electric Light Co.
	1893	Thomaston & Warren Light & Power Co.
	1893	Rockland & Thomaston Gas Light Co.
	1891	Rockland Electric Light & Gas Power Co.
1921		Kennebec Gas & Fuel Company
1921		Readfield Light & Power Company
1921		Winthrop & Wayne Light & Power Company
1921		Oxford Electric Company
	1916	Norway & Paris Street Railway (Name changed to Oxford Electric Co.)
	1905	Oxford Light Company
	1914	Maine Power Company
	1916	Mechanic Falls Electric Light Company
1921		Yarmouth Electric Company
1921		Maine Power Corp.
1921		Robinson Land Company
1922		Monmouth Electric Company
1922		Freeport Electric Light, Heat & Power Co.
1924		Lincoln County Power Company
	1917	Twin Village Water Co. (Previously leased)
	1916	Portland Power Development Company (Reorganized and incorporated as Lincoln County Power Company)

Year to CMP	Year to Predecessor	
	1918	Boothbay Harbor Electric Light & Power Co.
1924		Belgrade Power Company (Charles A. Hill)
1927		Western Maine Power Company
	1916	Limerick Water & Electric Company (Name changed to Western Maine Power Co.)
	1916	Steep Falls Light Company
	1917	Hiram Water, Light & Power Company
	1918	Denmark Light & Power Company
	1923	Bridgton Water & Electric Company
	1903	Bridgton Water Company
	1903	Bridgton & Harrison Electric Company
1927		Fryeburg Electric Company
1927		Bethel Light Company
1927		Black Stream Electric Company
1935		Androscoggin Electric Corporation
	1935	Androscoggin Electric Company
	1914	Lewiston & Auburn Electric Light Co.
	1914	Portland-Lewiston Interurban Railway
	1914	Portland, Gray & Lewiston Railway Co. (Name changed to Portland-Lewiston Interurban Railway, 1914)
	1935	Livermore Falls Light & Power Company
	1935	Turner Light & Power Company
1935		Dennistown Power Company
1935		Waterford Light & Power Company
1935		Central Securities Corporation
	1920	Georges River Power Company
	1931	Little Androscoggin Water Power Company
1940		Mount Vernon Light & Power Co. (Distribution Plant Only)
1941		Crawford Electric Company (Part of Distribution System Only)
1942		Cumberland County Power & Light Company
	1910	Cumberland Construction Company
	1912	Portland Electric Company
	1912	Consolidated Electric Light Co. of Maine
	1906	Buxton Construction Company
		Buxton & Hollis Power Company
	1912	Portland Lighting & Power Company
	1901	Cumberland Illuminating Company
	1901	Sebago Power Company
	1901	Deering Electric Company
	1901	Portland Electric Light Company
	1923	Westbrook Electric Company
	1923	York County Power Company
	1913	Ossippee Valley Power Company

Year to CMP	Year to Predecessor	
	1911	Sanford Light & Power Company
	1914	York Light & Heat Company
	1891	Biddeford & Saco Light & Power Co.
	1891	Saco & Biddeford Gas Light Co.
	1904	Old Orchard Electric Light Company
	1910	Agamenticus Electric Light Company
	1910	Agamenticus Light & Power Company
	1910	Kennebunk Electric Company
	1910	Wells Electric Light & Power Company
	1930	Pepperell Purchase (Certain Property & Rights)
	1930	Clark Power Company
	1931	Mallison Power Company
	1938	Berwick & Salmon Falls Electric Company
1945		White Mountain Power Company (Part of Distribution Plant Only)
1946		Consumers Electric Company
1947		Bryant Pond Electric Light Company (Distribution Plant Only)
1954		Crawford Electric Company
1958		Rumford Light Co.
1964		Monson Light & Power Co.
1965		Cornish & Kezar Falls Light & Power Co.
1965		Casco Bay Light & Power Co.
1966		Maine Consolidated Power Co.
1966		Phillips Electric
1976		Squirrel Island Village Corporation
1976		Rangeley Power Company
1981		Carrabasset Light & Power Company
1981		Maine portions of Public Service Company of New Hampshire service area, along the state border in York and Oxford Counties from Kittery to Upton, transferred to CMP

CMP generation assets, spring 1999

HYDRO (31 stations)

Station	Location	Units	Winter[i] Capacity, MW	Built[ii]
Kennebec River				
Harris	Indian Pond Twp. – Chase Stream Twp.[iii]	4	88	1954
W.S. Wyman	Moscow — Pleasant Ridge Plntn.	3	81	1930
Williams	Solon — Embden	2	15	1939
Weston	Skowhegan	4	13	1920
Shawmut	Fairfield — Benton	8	10	1913
Lockwood (50%)	Waterville — Winslow	7	4	1920
Messalonskee Stream				
Oakland (M-2)	Oakland	1	3	1901
Rice Rips (M-3)	Oakland	1	2	1908
Union Gas (M-5)	Waterville	1	2	1924
Sebasticook River				
Fort Halifax	Winslow	2	2	1908
Androscoggin River				
Gulf Island	Lewiston — Auburn	3	23	1926
Deer Rips	Auburn	7	7	1903
Androscoggin-3	Lewiston	1	4	1928
Monty	Lewiston — Auburn	2	28	1990
Brunswick	Brunswick — Topsham	3	20	1982
Lewiston Canal System				
Bates Upper	Lewiston	3	3	1912
Hill Mill	"	6	2	1922
Lower Androscoggin	"	1	—	1950
Bates Lower	"	1	—	Ca. 1915
Continental	"	5	1	1920
Saco River				
Hiram	Hiram — Baldwin	2	12	1917
Bonny Eagle	Standish — Hollis	6	10	1910
West Buxton	Buxton — Hollis	6	7	1907
Bar Mills	Buxton — Hollis	2	4	1956
Skelton	Buxton — Dayton	2	20	1948
Cataract	Biddeford — Saco	1	8	1937
NKL	Saco	2	1	Not certain[iv]

Presumpscot River

North Gorham	Gorham — Windham	2	2	1901

Ossipee River

Upper Kezar Falls	Parsonsfield — Porter	1	—	1941
Lower Kezar Falls	"	2	1	1984

Little Ossippee River

Ledgemere	Limerick — Waterboro	1	—	1984

FOSSIL

W.F. Wyman	Yarmouth	4	847*	1957-78
Mason	Wiscasset	5**	145	1942-55
Cape	Portland	2	42	1970

* CMP owned all of W.F. Wyman Units 1-3, but only 594 MW of the 620 MW, jointly built Unit 4.
** Mason Units 1-2 were deactivated in 1981; Units 3-5, deactivated in 1991, were returned to service to help meet regional power demand in 1997.

BIOMASS (wood chips, sawmill residue)

Aroostook Valley Electric Co. (former non-utility generator)	Fort Fairfield (Aroostook County, outside CMP's retail service area)	1	31	1987 (Acquired by CMP 1994)

NUCLEAR INTERESTS (Partial interests)

Millstone 3 (2.5% CMP)	Waterford, Connecticut	1	29	1986
Vermont Yankee (3.6% CMP)	Vernon, Vermont	1	19	1972

POWER-PURCHASE CONTRACTS

(Various)	Maine (67), Quebec (1)	68 NUG, etc.	574	(Various)

i. A null winter hydro capacity (—) indicates a solid freeze on that stream, with generation occurring in non-winter months. Current capacities may differ from historic numbers in text.
ii. As hydroelectric station; some dams were built earlier as sources of mechanical water power.
iii. Where a stream serves as a municipal boundary, both sides of the hydroelectric site are indicated.
iv. Acquired from industrial firm; records incomplete.

Sources: "Information Memorandum: Purchase of Generation Assets, June 1997," for unit data; CMP's 1998 FERC Form 1 Report for construction dates; CMP Property Tax Department.
Background: On April 7, 1999, CMP complied with Maine's new law on energy deregulation and completed the sale of 1,185 MW of generating capacity to FPL Energy, a subsidiary of Florida's FPL Group, Inc. Efforts to sell the remaining generation-related assets - Cape Station, the nuclear interests, an interest in a Hydro-Quebec transmission line terminating in Massachusetts, and energy associated with the purchased-power contracts — were under way as this book went to press.

CMP customers and energy sales

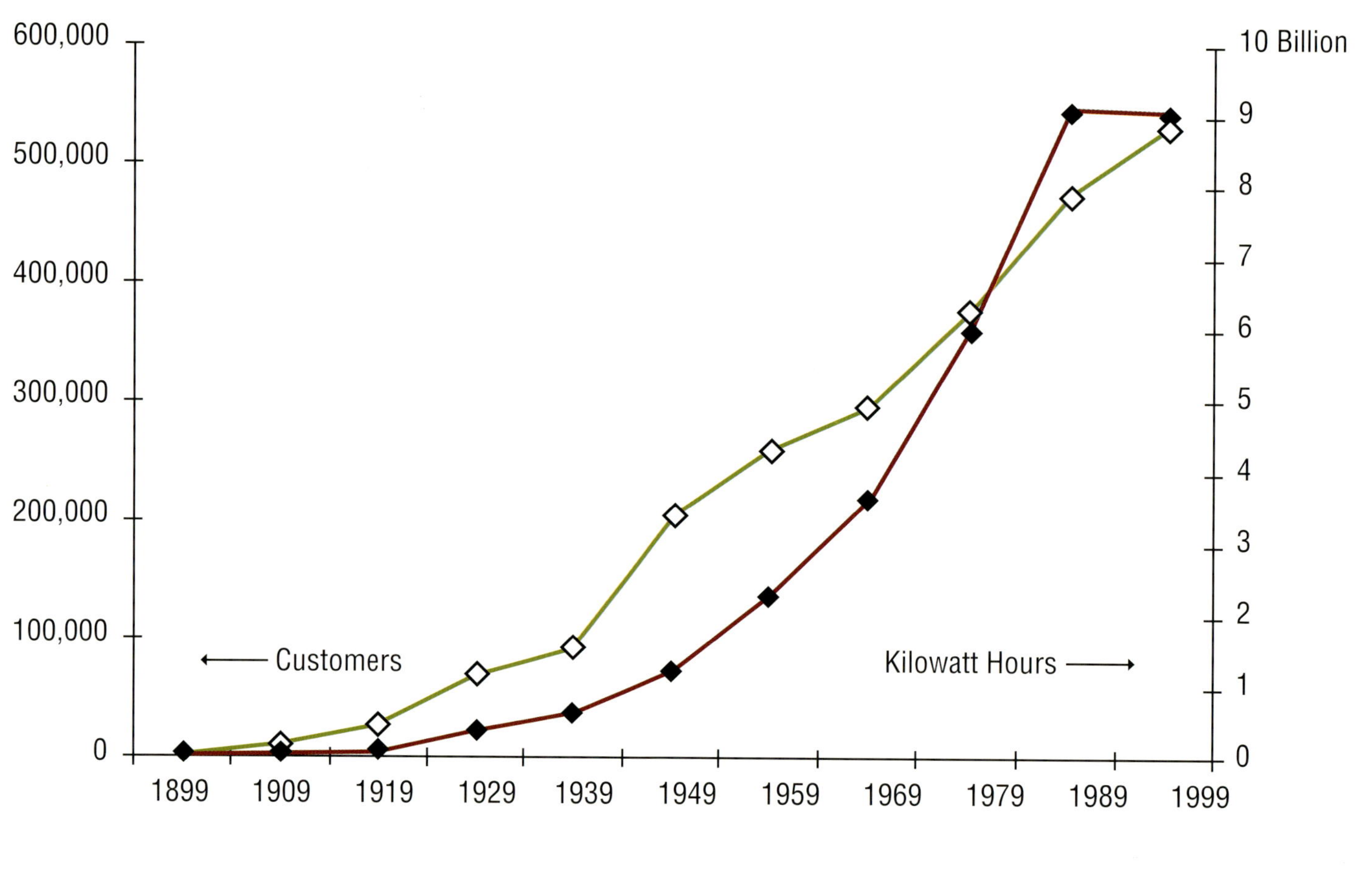

Customers and percent of sales, 1998

	Number of customers	Percent of sales
Residential	475,808	30
Commercial & industrial	53,527	67
Electric utilities	3	2
Street & area lighting	497	<1

Credits

Writing/editing	Clark Irwin
Design	David Guillemette
Page design	Susan Couture, Letter Systems
Images	CMP Archives; as indicated, Corbis Corporation, Blethen Maine Newspapers
Image support	Brad Ames, Walter Hanson, Khanh Vo; Rob Verrier, Ion Designs
Archival support	Kevin Bonner; Nancy McGinnis, Hubbard Free Library, Hallowell, Maine
Manuscript review	Arthur Adelberg, William Finn, Kathleen Newman; Victor Schlich

The text of this volume was composed
in Garamond Light and Helvetica Condensed
and printed by Letter Systems/Knowlton & McLeary
in Farmington, Maine, on Consort Royale Silk Tint.
The binding was executed by New Hampshire Bindery
in Concord, New Hampshire.

Lighting-upgrade project brightens
Middle Street, Portland, early 1950s